IGN TOURING AND LEISURE GUIDES

THE LOIRE

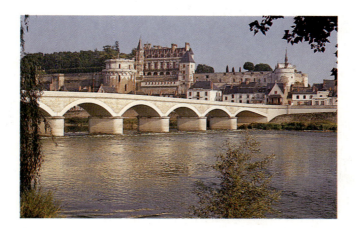

This guidebook forms part of a new series of regional touring and leisure guides to France and is produced in association with the French national mapping agency, the Institut Géographique National.

Feature articles trace the history, culture and architecture of each region and detail the prime sports and leisure pursuits available to holidaymakers. These are complemented by a gazetteer section which provides information on resorts and places of interest.

Through the exclusive use of IGN's superb topographical mapping, the motoring tours and walks outlined in each guide aim to help you discover new aspects of France. Above all, though, it is our hope that these guides open the door to your own discoveries.

Published by McCarta in association with
the INSTITUT GEOGRAPHIQUE NATIONAL

First published in 1992 by
McCarta Limited
15 Highbury Place
London N5 1QP

in association with

Institut Géographique National
136 bis, rue de Grenelle
75700 Paris

© Text and artwork, McCarta
© Maps, Institut Géographique National

Publishing Director Henderson McCartney
IGN Coordinator Nathalie Marthe
Series Editor Catharine Hutton
Project Coordinators Folly Marland, Ruth Keshishian
Editors Christian Senan, Daphne Terry, Lesley Young
Contributor Catherine Bray
Series Art Director Prue Bucknall
Designer Colin Lewis
Line maps and illustrations Paul Bryant
Translation Helen McPhail, Simon Knight
Research Pierre Janin, Stephane Chemouilli
Photo Research Christine Altur
Typeset by Columns Limited, Reading
Printed and bound by Grafedit, SpA. Bergamo, Italy

This book is sold subject to the condition that it shall not, by way of trade or otherwise, be lent, resold, hired out, or otherwise circulated without the publisher's consent in any form of binding or cover other than that in which it is published and without a similar condition including this condition being imposed on the subsequent purchaser.

British Library Cataloguing in Publication Data
The Loire — (IGN touring and leisure guides)
1. France. Loire Valley. Visitors' guides
I. Institut Géographique National
II. Series
914.4504839

ISBN 1-85365-283-5

Every care has been taken to ensure that all the information in this book is accurate. The publishers cannot accept any responsibility for any errors that may appear, or their consequences.

Photographic credits

Ancient Art and Architecture Collection R. Sheridan 66. **Buddy Bombard Society** 5. **C.D.T. Anjou** A. Choplain 19, 103. **C.D.T. Loir-et-Cher** 29 (*top*), 44, 58. **C.R.T. et des Loisirs** 46 (*top*), 63 (*bottom*), 70, 74. **Château Accueil** L. Falk 115 (*top*), D. Aubry 115 (*bottom*). **Club d'Ardrée** 33. **Club les Dryades** 32. **Domaine des Barres** 85. **Explorer** 11, 23, 24, 25, 93. Augustine 92. Bostian 68. C. Delu 72. J. Dupont 1, 17, 75, 89. C. Errath 13. S. Grandadam 88. F. Jalain 9, 12, 51 (*bottom*), 60, 62, 65, 104, 106, 107, 117. Jean-Paul 7, 22, 55, 71, 82, 91, 96, 102, 116. P. Maille 46 (*bottom*), 69. D. Mar 99. A. Martin 20. J. Nacivet 16, 43, 50, 51 (*top*), 109. P. Paillard 28. P. Plisson 49, 97. B. Rebouleau 73. P. Roy 8, 67, 95. F. Tetefolle 26, 54. N. Thibaut 77, 83, 100. A. Thomas 63 (*top*), 78. H. Veiller 41, 53, 76. P. Wysocki 64. **French Government Tourist Office (UK)** 110. **Gîtes de France (UK)** 111, 112. **Image Bank** D. Hamilton 80, 81. **Landscape Only** C. Waite 87. **Moulin Etape** 113. **J. Rizvi** 47. **Sheridan** B. Norman 90. **D. Terry** 4, 15.

CONTENTS

AN INTRODUCTION TO THE LOIRE 5
River landscapes 6
The Royal Val de Loire 10
Art and Literature 12
Châteaux of the Loire 14
Food and Wine 22

LEISURE ACTIVITIES 27
Outdoor leisure 28
Golf 30
Vineyards 34
Motoring tours 38
Walks 54

GAZETTEER 65

PRACTICAL INFORMATION 108

WHERE TO STAY 110

ATLAS 117

INDEX 144

AN INTRODUCTION TO THE LOIRE

For almost two hundred years, the kings of France chose to live in this region. At their invitation Flemish and Italian craftsmen were commissioned to enrich the arts of architecture, sculpture and painting of the period, in so doing creating some of the most beautiful buildings in the world and establishing the Loire valley as the very cradle of the Renaissance movement.

Hand in hand with the artistic nurturing of the countryside has gone the cultivation of the vine. Local wines which have inspired a rich, inventive cuisine; which have stimulated the imaginations of poets and writers, from Rabelais to Balzac; wines which today feature prominently on the lists of the best restaurants of the world.

If the history of the Loire valley is anything, it is the chronicle of the conspiracies and power struggles of France itself. An exceptional region – blessed both by nature and the efforts of men – here is to be found the very heart of France.

TITLE PAGE AMBOISE CHATEAU
LEFT EVENING AT AZAY-LE-RIDEAU
ABOVE HOT AIR BALLOON AT AMBOISE

RIVER LANDSCAPES

IMAGES ALONG THE WATER'S EDGE

According to etymologists, the name of the River Loire refers both to the cloudy waters along its banks and around its sandbanks and islands and to the mingled elements of its diverse nature. In the course of its 1,012-km journey the Loire embraces the waters of eleven tributaries, forming a vast catchment area which drains and irrigates 25 *départements*, like an enormous tree sprawling across the map of France. From its source at Mont-Gerbier-des-Joncs in Ardèche it makes its way through the gorges of the Massif Central and on across the plains beneath the Burgundy hillsides until it reaches its full breadth at Gien. This is where the Val de Loire begins, the Loire Valley which reveals the river in its fullest grandeur. Beyond Angers the Loire flows through the Armorican massif and down to the Atlantic Ocean.

For two hundred years the story of the Loire was the story of France herself; the great river enjoyed its own romantic era when, from 1829 onwards, dandies and writers embarked on steam barges to cruise down the river in their search for melancholy mists and poetic landscapes.

Its longest period of dominance, however, was in its commercial age: from ancient times until the beginning of the 19th century the Loire was France's major trade route, the main artery feeding and sustaining France. Riverside timber was destined, inevitably but honourably, to end as barrels or boats; fishing boats brought live catches from the Atlantic or from the inland waters of the Sologne; boats laden with fruits from the orchards, olives and figs, apples, nuts and cherries; traders' boats piled high with crockery and glass, crates of paper, gun flints, hawks and horses.

Today, with trade using other routes, the river is restored to fishermen, and the surrounding woods are prized for hunting. The riverside flora and fauna delight walkers and nature-lovers. Along its edge, forests of elm and oak shelter wild boar and deer; the woods, fields and heathlands are home to hare and pheasant, partridge and woodcock; grey heron stalk stiffly along the wooded banks while the islands are busy with colonies of beaver, and on the mudbanks sandpipers mingle with curlew. In winter, Bewick swans return and join the ospreys on the open waters.

❶ The Berry

This region of widely varying landscape is enclosed by the Loire on its eastern edge, the Sologne to the north, and the Creuse to the west. A score of châteaux and palaces stand along the banks of a dozen rivers, amongst them the Cher and the Indre, tributaries of the Loire which give their names to the two Berry *départements*.

To the east the slate roofs of the Sancerre villages lie beneath hillsides laden with vines. This is the starting point for the Sauvignon wine route, a variety of grape favoured in the vineyards along Berry's northern fringe: Sancerre, Menetou-Salon, Quincy, Reuilly.

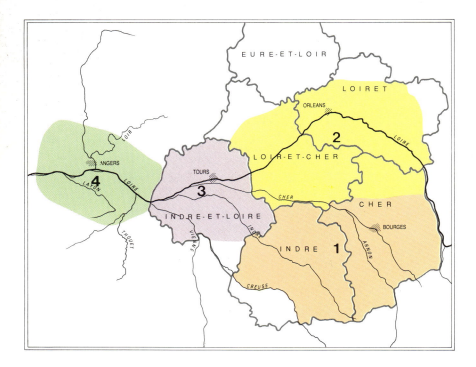

Boischaut to the south lies astride the River Indre, with its picturesque settings of alternating woodland pastures and valleys. This is a landscape 'which can only be seen by peering between the branches', George Sand's proud and mysterious land with its pale or dark stone châteaux offering an early hint of the neighbouring Pays d'Oc.

The well-stocked *étangs* or fishing pools of the thousand square kilometre Brenne area to the west are surrounded by forests and heathland with abundant game. Keen photographers as well as those seeking the out-of-the-ordinary should visit the Haute-Touche animal reserve adjacent to the château of Azay-le-Ferron, in order to observe the magnificent wildlife living free in the reserve's 450 hectares.

*For further details of the Haute-Touche Nature Reserve contact **Azay-le-Ferron** ☎ 54.39.23.43 and for walks in **Boischaut** contact the Tourist Office at La Châtre ☎ 54.48.22.64.*

❷ Orléanais and Blésois

Apart from the Sologne in the south and the Forêt d'Orléans in the north, the region is given over to farming. The Gâtinais, to the east, is an area of small-scale farming, livestock, and beekeeping. To the west, the vast rich plains of the Grande Beauce produce abundant cereal crops, while the neighbouring Petite Beauce is more undulating and less rich, bordering on the little fields, woodlands and rich pastures of the Perche area.

The Loire Valley proper is the 10-km-broad centre of the region which corresponds to the *départements* of Loiret and Loir-et-Cher; this is its richest stretch, containing the twenty-five most important châteaux. Dropping down from the hills of the Bourbonnais and the Nivernais, the river eases into a broad shallow valley, its curves extending to the horizon under soft light. The silvery green of poplars and willows is reflected in the blue-grey of gravel-pits with occasional ochre flashes of pale sand.

A few kilometres upstream from Gien, the canal aqueduct at Briare is the first great bridge over the river. Built by Gustave Eiffel between 1890 and 1897 and 664 metres long, the bridge is lit by filigree lamps which contrast sharply with the massive Egyptian-style lamp standards at each end of the bridge.

The wide bend of the river from Gien to Blois, with the Sologne lying within the curve, marks the beginning of the sequence of châteaux, parks, gardens, nursery-gardens, and horticulture of all kinds. Châteauneuf-sur-Loire has a 19th-century English park, blending the rare scents of Florida dogwoods and Chinese black cypress with native elms and poplar trees and a colourful undergrowth of giant rhododendrons.

North of Orléans lies the immense state forest of 140,000 hectares, where in summer one can find freshness in the shade of the centuries-old elms and oaks, and pools either used for leisure pursuits or left as the wilderness home of deer and boar. To the south the first ripples of the River Loiret appear deep in the botanical park of Orléans-la-Source, amid flowery mosaics dominated by roses, rhododendrons and irises at the foot of a modest château.

The Sologne, further to the south, may seem the wildest of landscapes yet it owes its riches to human hands. This once unhealthy marshland was drained and replanted a century ago. Today, tracks of pale sand thread their way through a forest of 180,000 hectares – pines, oaks, chestnuts and birches standing in an undergrowth of heather, often concealing boar or deer. The marshes are now pools full of fish, the chosen haunt of woodcock and mallard. The charm and mystery of this hunters' paradise was also the setting chosen by Alain-Fournier for his famous novel *Le Grand Meaulnes*. The few villages, Romorantin-Lanthenay for example, seem to hide like birds in their nests, as discreet and shy as young fledglings. The houses of the little town lie astride the branches

THE LOIRE AT GIEN

of the River Sauldre as it winds and twists to form little islands.

At Meung-sur-Loire, between Orléans and Beaugency, the waters divide into delicate streams running off the Beauce plateau, converging here to be absorbed by the river; the timeless charm of the little town is enhanced by several old mills along the banks of the clear rivulets known as Les Mauves.

Several hectares of horticultural cultivation scent the air beyond Beaugency and around St-Laurent-des-Eaux, turning in the autumn to vast panoramas of curving foliage.

Where the River Cher flows into the Loire

near Villandry the river itself has constructed its own delightful designs, in the form of the underground landscape around Savonnières. Filtering through the rock, the river has carved out caves and labyrinthine galleries punctuated by waterfalls and lakes. The calcifying powers of the limestone water have created a magical and surreal world of stalactites and stalagmites. Here prehistoric fauna are frozen into crystalline luminescence in a Gallo-Roman burial ground where fantastically shaped creatures gleam among the windings of the underground maze.

Out in the open the River Cher 'flows past gardens, goats, and fields', according to the writer Gilbert Cesbron. Between the Cher and the Indre, in Champeigne, the River Indrois has carved out its own valley. Between modest hills criss-crossed with tracks winding through shady copses, it twists between Romanesque churches and monasteries, past manors and romantic country houses.

The Indre valley is a land of osiers, and where it meets the Loire the larger river has 'plump islands with reed-beds fat with sap'. The muddy fields clinging to the winding banks of the river bristle with the tall plumes. Cut and trussed in winter, the reeds remain in water until the spring, to mature; then, stripped of their husk and dried, they are ready for use. The craft of wickerwork is practised in Villaines-les-Rocher, the cane-workers' and basket-makers' town to the south of Azay-le-Rideau. The 'black' and 'grey' reeds are woven on the ground, following long-established tradition.

Where the Vienne and the Indre valleys meet, to the south-east, the Sainte-Maure plateau rears up, streaked with small water-courses and a few pools. Its sand and fossilized shells were laid down in the Faluns sea in the Tertiary era.

Opening dates and times of **Park of Orléans-la-Source** *1 Apr–11 Nov, daily 9–6. 12 Nov–31 Mar, daily 2–6. The* **Savonnières caves**: *8 Feb–31 Mar, daily 9–12 and 2–6.30. 1 Apr–14 Oct, daily 9–7. 16 Oct–20 Dec, daily 9–12 and 2–6.*

❸ The Touraine

This region makes up the major portion of the *département* of Indre-et-Loire. The Loire, now some 1.5 to 2 kilometres wide, winds round islets of sand planted with poplar and willow. The great vineyards of Touraine can be seen on the upper slopes round Bourgueil, Chinon and Tours, while the lower hillsides are the domain of early vegetables – the celebrated local asparagus is cultivated on these alluvial sands. One after another the Cher, the Indre and the Vienne pour into the Loire, creating prosperous valleys of orchards and rich pastures along their course.

The area known as the Gâtine Tourangelle lies to the north, between the rivers Loir and Loire. From Vendôme to Tours numerous *habitations troglodytiques* or cave dwellings are to be found.

Though these types of dwelling were first used as places of hiding during the days of barbarian invasions, then again in the medieval wars, their use as permanent homes has persisted down the centuries. Houses carved out of the rock produced an important additional resource – the sale of the stone extracted. For as the writer Théophile Gautier remarked, 'each house hollowed out produces another one constructed'. Nowadays many of them have been converted, with wine and mushrooms benefiting from the steady 13-degree temperature of the caves.

The strange Chinese silhouette which appears on the edge of the forest in the valley, down-river from Amboise, is the Chanteloup pagoda, the last remaining vestige of a now-lost château built by Louis XV's minister the Duke de Choiseul. Standing by a stretch of water, the six-storey edifice is decorated with carved symbols of dedication to Friendship. Each storey consists of a circular domed room, with the final one, 44 metres above the ground, providing a spectacular viewing point.

Opening dates and times of the **Chanteloup Pagoda**: *1 Apr–30 Sep, daily except Mon 9–12 and 2–6.*

THE LOIRE AT LANGEAIS

RIVER LANDSCAPES

SANDBANKS, INDRE-ET-LOIRE

❹ The Anjou

Anjou begins at Montsoreau. It can be regarded as two provinces, for, following the boundaries between the great groups of vineyards, there is first White Anjou to the east, corresponding to the Saumur region with its woods and heathland and broad plains edged with chalky hill slopes. Then to the west is the rolling landscape of Black Anjou, dark schist soil with small fields, thick copses, and slate quarries.

The soft contours of the valleys of Anjou continue the gentle rolling hills of the Touraine in an alternating patchwork of flowery meadows and woods of oak and chestnut. And as ever the river flows on through what the poet Du Bellay called 'la douceur angevine', Anjou's distinctive sweet mildness. To the south-east, between the rivers Aubance, Layon, Thouet and Loire, the village of Doué-la-Fontaine is the centre of a group of strange cave dwellings, hollowed out of the white chalky hillsides.

One such dwelling, at Donezé-sur-Doué, has a broad band of individual portrait figures sculpted in the round, probably by a brotherhood of 16th-century stone-masons who may have lived here. The underground village of Rochemenier nearby, consisting of several farmhouses and a chapel, is now a museum of this distinctive way of life, and displays many of the everyday possessions of 19th-century peasants.

Visitors to north-west Anjou will be fascinated by a different kind of underground landscape where, in the 126-metre-deep 'Mine Bleue' or Blue Mine near Noyant-la-Gravoyère – the only one of its kind in France – they can explore the magical surroundings of the slate caves of St-Blaise.

Opening dates and times of the **Rochemenier Village Museum**: 1 Apr-30 Jun and 1-31 Sep, daily except Mon 9.30–12 and 2–7. 1 Jul-31 Aug, daily 9.30–12 and 2–7. 1-31 Oct, daily 2–7. 1 Nov-31 Mar, Sat and Sun 2–7.

For all details of the **Blue Mine at St-Blaise** contact the Tourist Office at Angers ☎ 41.88.69.93.

An uncertain future

Irregularity and unpredictability are the characteristics of the noble River Loire. The impermeable soils through which it flows and the absence of regulatory barriers leave it dependent on the vagaries of the weather. Periods of flood when the river rushes into valleys alternate with periods of low water when vast sand banks are exposed and the river is left as a mere thread. Both extremes are the combined result of the Mediterranean climate upstream and the Atlantic influence downstream. Although the farming populace fears prolonged periods of low water above all, the rarer flash-floods are more disastrous; on average these occur four times each century, carrying as much as 6000–9000 cubic metres of water per second at their peak. Massive sand-quarrying activities along the river banks create a series of deep gorges which further accentuate this dangerous down-flow.

Historically the Loire was the first river to be controlled, though it has never really been tamed; protective works began in the 9th century under Louis le Debonnaire who ordered the building of the first *turcies* or dykes. In the 12th century Authion had its first dyke, and these earthworks restricting the Loire were extended until it was corseted for 530 km, from Decize to Nantes. The dykes could not, however, always withstand the exceptional floods of the capricious river, which would burst through and drown everything in its passage. In the 17th century Colbert had the dykes raised by 7 metres, and in the following century any which had been submerged were raised yet again. These survived until the extreme floods of the 19th century which burst out inexorably in 1846, 1856 and 1866. It was during this distressing period that the engineer Guillaume Comoy demonstrated the need to control the areas of steepest flow.

To prevent further catastrophes and to regulate the down-flow, dams and reservoirs were built at Villarest upstream from Roanne, at Naussac on the River Allier, and on the River Donezau in the Allier basin. Others are planned at Veuldre-sur-l'Allier, 50 km from Nevers, at Serre-de-la-Farre in Haute-Loire, and at Chambonchard on the River Cher, and there are also plans to strengthen the dykes.

These problems are the responsibility of the EPALA (Establissement Public pour l'Aménagement de la Loire et de ses Affluents). Surveys and statistical models make it clear that these great floods will occur again and that the consequences, in valleys which are still exposed to flooding and which are increasingly urbanized, will be catastrophic. However, ecologists have no wish to see the river imprisoned and stagnant and open to rapid pollution. Is there an appropriate solution? So far none has been found, and the river's future remains uncertain.

THE ROYAL VAL DE LOIRE

KINGS, QUEENS AND COURTESANS

In May 1152 the Plantagenet King Henry II (1133–1189, son of the Count of Anjou and Maine and his wife the heiress of Normandy and England), married Eleanor of Aquitaine. In view of her vast dowry which included the French lands of Poitou, Aquitaine and Gascony, it is not difficult to understand why the man who two years later was to become king of England was not over-concerned about his future wife's reputation (she had been repudiated by the French king, Louis VII, because of her notorious infidelity during her absence on interminable crusades). Twenty years later, however, Henry chose to keep Eleanor in close seclusion at Winchester for sixteen years rather than lose her great dowry by repudiating her in his turn. The enchanting Eleanor was thus married to first one and then the other of the two protagonists involved in the war between France and Anjou which lasted from 1159 until 1299; this was the first stage of the Hundred Years' War, with the second stage following in the next century, from 1337 to 1453. Throughout the sequence of broken treaties and offensives punctuated by periods of truce, the Loire Valley changed hands continually, and was part of the stakes which were to turn the English and the French into hereditary enemies.

Joan of Arc and the 'King of Bourges'

In March 1429 Joan of Arc (1412–1431) arrived in Chinon, home of Charles VII (1403–1461), who since his flight from Paris was referred to, slightingly, as 'The King of Bourges'. The 17-year-old girl, dressed like a man in breeches and jerkin, claimed to have been sent by God to save France and the French king. In April Joan, 'La Pucelle' or 'The Virgin', was appointed head of the royal armies, and had armour and banners made for herself in Tours. Her faith galvanized the French army into liberating Orléans, besieged by the English, and gradually opened up the road to Rheims where Charles VII was crowned on 17 July 1429. In September the army was demobilized and Joan, who had sworn to 'kick the English out of France' was forced to continue the struggle with reduced forces. Imprisoned at Compiègne eight months later, she was betrayed to the English by the Burgundians. Condemned to death, she was executed at Rouen in May 1431.

A romantic interlude

Charles VII gave Agnès Sorel (1422–1449), who became his mistress in 1444, the estate of Beauté 'so that she should be the Dame de Beauté in name as well as in fact'. Although the bishop Thomas Belin records that she was 'a pretty enough bitch', and contemporary chronicles commented that she wore excessively low-cut dresses, she appears in Fouquet's painting as the Madonna, and the secular version (of which Loches has a copy) still bears witness to her charms. Her effigy, which is nonetheless seductive for being part of her tomb, is equally attractive, and it is easy to imagine the embarrassment of the canons of St-Ours church, who for three hundred years sought to rid themselves of the sinner's monument. The king's treasurer, Jacques Coeur, was accused of poisoning her on behalf of the future Louis XI, son of Charles VII, who hated her.

Marriage manoeuvres

Charles VIII (1470–1498), son of Louis XI, was twenty in 1490 when the 17-year-old Duchess of Brittany was married by proxy to Maximilian of Austria, who thus had France in a pincer-grip on three frontiers. To forestall this threat, Charles VIII declared war on Anne of Brittany, and in November 1491 the young duchess, at his mercy and under siege in Rennes, was forced to surrender, renouncing both her duchy and her marriage. A month later she married Charles in the château of Langeais.

In 1492 the young king, free from the guardianship of his sister Anne de Beaujeu, discovered simultaneously the delights of power and of marriage, but on 7 April 1496 he hit his head against the stone lintel of a low door and died the same day, leaving Anne a widow and childless despite her four pregnancies.

Anne's marriage contract provided that in the absence of a Dauphin (son of the reigning French king), she should marry the next in line to the throne; thus it was that the Duke of Orléans legitimately acquired the throne and the queen, both long coveted. However, the Duke – now Louis XII (1462–1515) – had first to annul his marriage to Jeanne 'the lame', daughter of Louis XI, in return for which the Pope Alexander Borgia demanded the dukedom of Valentinois and the hand of a French princess for his son. While Cesare Borgia, who was a cardinal, his sister's lover, and, it was said, his brother's murderer, married again at Chinon, Louis XII hastened to join Anne at Blois. He married the pretty widow without delay; ten years younger than Charles, he was attractive to women in his taste for the arts and lively intelligence. As a consequence of the marriage, Blois gained the pavilion which bears the queen's name, and a new main keep – but France still had no male heir, and their only daughter, Claude, was betrothed in 1506 to François, son of Charles d'Angoulême and Louise de Savoie, to retain the crown for the Valois.

François I: a brilliant king

Crowned in the spring of 1515, François I (1494–1547) was admired for his vitality and appetite, and his vigour brought renewed health to his exhausted kingdom. He committed his extraordinary energy in turn to fresh Italian campaigns and to the continuing building work at Blois and Amboise, where life revolved round festivities. This same insatiable appetite took him hunting for stag and boar and – fine ladies; 'I cannot help but love three of them', he wrote, referring to the gentle Claude, his wife, and to his mistresses, the dark Françoise de Foix and the blonde Anne de Pisseleu d'Helly. During these happy years, between 1515 and 1519, François could also take pride in his friendship with the great genius of the century, Leonardo da Vinci, who was his guest in the manor of Clos-Lucé. The magnificent old man designed costumes for masquerades and tournaments at the royal festivities, and created architectural designs which may have included Chambord (begun in 1519). Chambord was the king's passion, an enormous and fantastic château.

The revenge of Catherine de' Medici

When François I's successor, his son Henri II (1519–1559), came to the throne in 1547, he had already been married to Catherine de' Medici since 1533, and his meeting with Diane de Poitiers dated from four years later. Diane was the king's only lasting passion. Her beauty, outweighed in legend by her eternal youthfulness, inspired a score of statues and paintings from the greatest artists of the age. For some twenty years she was the most tenderly cherished woman in France, richer than the Queen herself. In 1555 Henri II gave her the

HENRI II

château of Chenonceau, and it is to her that we owe the astonishing inspiration of extending the main building by an elegant river bridge.

At the death of Diane's royal lover (Henri II was mortally wounded in a tournament), Catherine de' Medici took back Chenonceau which she had always coveted. After a brief stay at Chaumont-sur-Loire, Diane returned to her domain at Anet, given to her by the king in 1549. It was at this château in the *département* of Eure-et-Loir that the skills of Philibert Delorme were perhaps given the freest rein, the combined blend of his architectural talent and her feminine charm.

From François II to Henri III via Charles IX, Catherine de' Medici (1519–1589), acting as regent or counsellor to the king, brought all her weight to bear on the fate of France. She it was who strengthened the Catholic faction of the Guise family, in the hope of preserving the throne from the Protestant Prince de Condé or Henri de Navarre. For nearly thirty years the bloody Wars of Religion, into which France was plunged from 1560 to 1598, coincided with her dark reign.

The Amboise plot of March 1560 was the first Protestant attempt to overthrow François, Duke of Guise (1519–1563), and his brother Charles, Cardinal of Lorraine (1525–1574), to whom Catherine had entrusted power. The attack failed, and Amboise became a vast slaughterhouse: corpses hung from balconies, the courtyards ran with the blood of beheaded nobles, and the Loire swept away the bodies of the Huguenots. But two years later hostilities broke out again with the Duke of Guise's Vassy massacre. Massacre indeed became commonplace, 'cruelty beyond barbarity and inhumanity', on both sides. In 1572 came the Eve of St Bartholomew, when the assassination of Coligny – arranged by Catherine – marked the beginning of three days of uninterrupted slaughter. According to the poet Agrippa d'Aubigné, the River Loire ran red with blood.

A playhouse king

When Henri III (1551–1598) came to the throne in 1574, the Duke Henri le Balafré (1550–1588) and his brother, the cardinal Louis (1556–1588), confirmed the power of the Guise family. Henri III was a dressed-up homosexual, 'a scented flirt with gloved hands, who slept with his pugs and pet monkeys, a playhouse king bedecked with feathers and sparkling with rings', surrounded by his 'darlings', whose orgiastic feasts echoed round the salons of Chenonceau.

By 1588 Henri III was a figure of ridicule, liable to be overthrown at any moment in favour of his rival the powerful and revered Henri, Duke of Guise. In December he concluded that the duke must die, and set up a plot: on the morning of 13 December Henri de Guise came to the château at Blois to attend the Council in the king's apartments, where in a secluded room the gentlemen of the royal guard, the Forty-five, awaited him with their daggers. Alone against the guard, the Duke defended himself ferociously before falling victim to their attack. The king was waiting in his cabinet for news of this death and considered that his enemy was a 'long time dying'. His brother the Cardinal, locked up in the attics, was executed the next day, for which Henri III apologized by letter to the Pope.

The deaths of Catherine de' Medici in January 1589 and of Henri III in August of the same year (the latter assassinated by the monk Jacques Clément) left France in the hands of Henri of Navarre, who became Henri IV. He brought the Wars of Religion to an end in 1598 with the Edict of Nantes, and was in his turn stabbed to death by Ravaillac in 1610.

France had suffered continuous wars for two hundred years, and, apart from increased prosperity under François I, had lived in poverty and occasional famine throughout the two centuries: and yet it was in these same lands and times that the French artistic Renaissance was to flower and flourish.

ART AND LITERATURE

CRADLE OF THE FRENCH RENAISSANCE

Late in the 14th century the Duke Jean de Berry (1340–1416) preferred the delights of art and the pleasures of the aesthete to the vanities of power. His passion for collecting overwhelmed all other interests, and his 17 châteaux and great houses (Gien, Bourges, Mehun-sur-Yèvres, Saumur, etc.) were full of miniatures and precious stones from distant lands. As he moved from one château to another, the duke was always accompanied by his swans and his bears, as well as the 400 metres of tapestry which provided his domestic décor.

The Duke de Berry owned some twenty richly illuminated books of hours: Jacquemart de Hesdin created *Les Grandes Heures* and *Les Petites Heures*, their margins embellished with vivid scrolls of birds in soft and delicate colours. The masterpiece of the genre, however, was *Les Très Riches Heures*, created by Pol de Limbourg and his brothers, forerunners of the modern approach to painting, with suppleness and elegance breaking away from medieval stiffness. When this new richness and vigour in painting finally escaped from the constraint of books, the legacy of Limbourg's example was to be a tender spring-like clarity influenced by the graceful harmony which is characteristic of this part of France. It was in the Loire Valley that the French Renaissance blossomed, deriving its identity from the landscape itself, and retaining between the influences of Flemish realism and Italian idealism that intimate and colloquial poetic style which is its distinctive feature.

In 1495 Charles VIII brought back from Naples the architect Domenico Cortone, known as Le Boccator, the sculptor Guido Mazzoni, and Dom Pacello, landscape gardener. Under Louis XIII this Italian group increased steadily in number, including in particular Andrea Solario and Fra Giocondo. Châteaux were transformed into pleasure dwellings, their extensive forests used for hunting throughout the year. But it was for the women who offered the kings the pleasures of the mind and of the flesh that the châteaux were embellished with lacy stonework, and it was to shed light on their beauty that the sombre façades of the fortresses were pierced with airy windows. At Blois as at Amboise the combination of Italian and French master-craftsmen created a balance, blending purity of line with richness of ornamentation.

The French Renaissance took hold in the reign of François I, who renewed the links with Italy. He attracted many artists to his court: Benvenuto Cellini, Leonardo da Vinci, Andrea del Sarto, Iacopo de' Rossi, Primaticcio, and Niccolo del Abbato. The official court painters remained French, however; it was Jean Clouet (1475–1541) followed by his son François Clouet (1520–1572) who painted the portraits of the kings, queens, princes and favourites. Close concentration and uncompromising psychological analysis are the characteristics of this school of painting, which inherited from the North, Jean Clouet's home-land, the precision of the miniaturist.

The paintings on the theme of 'ladies at their toilette' (1550–1600) are lovers' gifts to the kings from the royal favourites. The nudes are tactfully un-named, but the sumptuous surroundings and haughty attitude of the models hint that the subjects were Françoise de Châteaubriand, Anne de Pisseleu, Diane de Poitiers, and the beauties of Catherine de' Medici's 'flying squad', who, like Agnès Sorel before them and Gabrielle d'Estrées afterwards, also revealed their 'anonymous' loveliness.

The other two great French artists of the end of the century were sculptors: Jean Goujon (1540–1560), and Germain Pilon (1560–1590). The soft folds and supple limbs of their work are further reminders of the inspiration flowing from the Loire and the cool freshness of its rivers and forests.

SOME LITERARY LIGHTS

Rabelais: Lover of life

One of the two houses owned by the lawyer Antoine Rabelais, father of the writer, still survives – La Devinière, 7 km from Chinon; it was in Chinon and the surrounding countryside that the young François Rabelais (1494–1533) grew up. He attempted the religious life and then studied medicine before discovering his true vocation as a writer. *Pantagruel*, published in 1532, marked the beginning of an epic of good eating and drinking around Chinon: 'Chinon, Chinon, a little town that boasts a name of great renown: High on the rock its ramparts show, with woods above and the Vienne below' sings Pantagruel. The memorable excesses of Gargantua and Pantagruel were no more than the literary exaggerations of

BIRTHPLACE OF RABELAIS

a strong appetite for the delectable produce of Touraine, and the episode of the 'dive bouteille' or 'bottle divine' is a form of homage to the much-appreciated Vouvray wines. La Devinière is now a museum of books and documents relating to Rabelais' life and work.
Opening dates and times of **Rabelais Museum**:
15 Mar-15 Sept, daily 9–12 and 2–6.
1 Oct-14 Mar, daily except Wed 9–12 and 2–5.
For all details of Rabelais tour, contact the Tourist Office at Chinon ☎ 47.98.40.91.

Ronsard: Poet of love

Born in the manor-house of La Possonnière, Pierre de Ronsard (1524–1585) took holy orders in 1543, not so much from religious conviction as from a need for material security. Posterity knows him as the founder of the group of poets calling themselves the *Pléiade*, and above all as a great poet of love and of women. The ethereal tones of his first *Amours* (1552), dedicated to the unattainable Cassandra Salviati, soon gave way to more down-to-earth yearnings; in *Continuation* (1556), inspired by the young and accessible peasant girl, Marie Dupin, sensuality replaced platonic love. The fresh spontaneity and poignant sincerity of Ronsard's writing marked a new beginning for French poetry. The poet's progress through the countryside from one priory to another can be traced in his evocative lines: 'There the trees of our forests reach up to the sky, There a thousand woods and a thousand meadows lie. There flow the babbling waters of a hundred thousand springs, There run a thousand rocky paths where sounding Echo rings, And answering my song of love, of love alone it sings ...'
Opening dates and times of **Ronsard Museum**, St Cosme Priory:
15 Mar-30 Apr and 1-30 Sep, daily except Wed 9–12 and 2–6.
1 Jul-31 Aug, daily except Wed 9–6.
1 Oct-14 Mar, daily except Wed 9–12 and 2–5.

Balzac and 'The Human Comedy'

The childhood of Honoré de Balzac (1799–1850) as a permanent boarder, neglected by his family, was divided between Tours, where he was born, Saint-Cyr, and Vendôme. His first years in Paris were scarcely happier, and the legal studies imposed on him by his parents ran strongly counter to his literary vocation.

Nonetheless Paris and the Loire Valley held equal sway in his heart as in his work, and he was drawn in turn to the worldly life of the capital and the calm sweetness of the banks of the Loire. These were the sources of his inspiration and energy for his titanic creation of almost a hundred novels, *La Comédie Humaine*.

It was to Saché that the literary giant retreated when weary between 1834 and 1848, to renew his strength – which was immediately consumed once more in his strenuous labours. He wrote: 'Do not ask me why I love Touraine ... I love it as an artist loves art.' It was on the banks of the River Indre that he discovered the setting for his novel of pure love, *Le Lys dans la Vallée*.

'There can be found a valley which seems to turn gold below the châteaux perched on the

BALZAC'S BEDROOM, SACHE

hills at either side; a magnificent emerald bowl with the Indre unrolling in sepentine windings along the bottom ... this long ribbon of water rippling in the sun between two green banks ... these lines of poplars, decorating this valley of love with their lacy movement ... the oak trees advancing between the vineyards along the banks where the river curves round, ever-changing, and ... these blurred horizons which retreat and confuse.'
Opening dates and times of **Balzac Museum**, Saché:
15 Mar-30 Jun and 1-30 Sep, daily 9–12 and 2–6.
1 Jul-31 Aug, daily 9–6.
1 Oct-14 Mar, daily except Wed 9–12 and 2.5.

George Sand: Herald of women's lib

The first woman writer to proclaim equality of the sexes in artistic matters, George Sand (1804–1876) – under her true name of Aurore Dupin – spent her childhood in the château of Nohant which became her home.

Her books, published between 1846 and 1853, *La Mare au Diable*, *François le Champi*, *La Petite Fadette* and *Les Maîtres Sonneurs*, are set in her beloved Berry countryside which she described so well: 'All the heights are wooded, giving our distant views their fine blue shade, which turns violet and almost black on stormy days' (*La Vallée Noire*). 'Anyone who plunges into these twisting narrow tracks that turn off the roads at any moment, to seek shade and silence, will quickly discover fresh calm landscapes, fields of tender green, melancholy streams, stands of alder and ash trees, a whole peaceful pastoral natural life' (*Valentine*).
Opening dates and times of **George Sand Museum**, Château de Nohant:
2 Jan-31 Mar and 16 Nov-31 Dec, daily 10–11.30 and 2–3.30.
1 Apr-30 Jun, daily 9–11.30 and 2–5.30.
1 Jul-15 Sep, daily 9–11.30 and 1.30–6.

The Loire Valley can claim in all some fifty famous writers who were either born in the area, sought refuge there, or came searching for a mainspring for their inspiration. For further information about their homes and their history, consult *Writers' France* by John Ardagh (Hamish Hamilton 1989).

CHATEAUX OF THE LOIRE
BUILDING ON THE GRAND SCALE

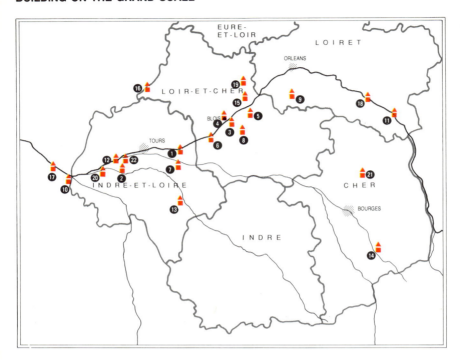

When Charles VIII came to the throne in 1492, he began transforming the former fortress of Amboise, where he was born, into a comfortable château. On his return from the Naples campaign he brought a number of Italian craftsmen with him to work on the Amboise improvements, and this handful of men was, indirectly, to trigger off the complete rebirth of French art, its Renaissance.

❶ Amboise

Although the basic style of the Amboise château is Flamboyant Gothic, the Italian influence can be seen in the decoration: the keystones of the Tour des Minimes arches are ornamented with dolphins, Medusa heads and grotesque faces; the pediment of the upper doorway of the Tour Heurtault bears decorative foliage and arabesque-carved pillars.

The medieval battlements and machicolations along the top of the right-angled royal keep are now mere symbols of warfare used for ornamentation, and the upper part of the façade is liberally studded with small dormer windows embellished with linked curving pinnacles. A carved lintel representing the conversion of St-Hubert, in the Flamboyant style chapel begun by Louis XI and completed by Charles VIII, is famous for its vivid and poetic expression.

François I spent his childhood in Amboise and enriched it in his turn, twenty years later, with a Renaissance wing which may owe something to Leonardo da Vinci's presence in the nearby Clos-Lucé.

Opening dates and times
2 Jan-6 Apr, daily 9–12 and 2–5.
1 Sep-31 Dec, daily 9–12 and 2–5.30.
7 Apr-30 Jun, daily 9–12 and 2–6.30.
1 Jul-31 Aug, daily 9–6.30.

❷ Azay-le Rideau

'A many-faceted diamond set in the River Indre on piles masked by flowers' – such was Balzac's description of the château of Azay-le-Rideau, justifying its reputation as the pearl among Loire châteaux; set among wooded hillsides, it stands on a small island surrounded by the waters of the Loire. The château was built between 1518 and 1527 for François I's silversmith, sire Gilles Berthelot, on the site of a former fortress destroyed by Charles VII. Designed for leisure, the château is outstanding for its fine Italian-influenced architecture. The façade's plain pillars and window-frames add to the contrasting delicacy of the ornamental carving; medieval-style machicolations become an embroidery emphasizing the luminosity of the third storey with its many dormer windows; the watch turrets on the corner towers add a note of grace to the blue-sheened slate roofs tapering skywards.

A particular feature of this château is the blend of simplicity with subtlety of detail. The elegant result is magnificently enhanced by its gleaming white tufa stone.

Rooms open to the public contain furniture, pictures and Renaissance objects; they include fine examples of Gobelins tapestry, and a period copy of a Jean Clouet painting showing

CHATEAUX OF THE LOIRE

EVENING AT AZAY-LE-RIDEAU

Gabrielle d'Estrées in her bath. And finally there is the famous grand staircase with its six flights of steps, and coffered ceiling emblazoned with royal medallions, adding as it were the flourish of a long stone signature to the whole edifice.

Opening dates and times
1 Oct-31 Mar, daily 10–12.15 and 2–4.45.
1 Apr-30 Jun and 1-30 Sep, daily 9.30–5.45.
1 Jul-31 Aug, daily 9.30–6.30.

❸ Beauregard

The château of Beauregard replaced an earlier hunting lodge belonging to François I on the edge of the forest of Russy. It was built between 1545 and 1553 by Jean de Thiers, Henri II's secretary of state, a shrewd and cultured man, a friend of the poet Ronsard.

Of modest dimensions, Beauregard consists of a central portion framed between two rectangular pavilions, which was extended by a further wing under Louis XIII. Its design, which was advanced for its day, corresponds to the principles of Serlio which were to become the basis of classical architecture: beauty and elegance stripped bare of all ornamental excess, expressive in its careful use of pure lines and perfect proportions. The only Renaissance indulgence is the line of dormer windows beneath a gable with grooved sloping sides. The coffered ceiling of Jean du Thiers' own Renaissance chamber or office is decorated with the emblem of the Thiers family 'azur à trois grelots d'or' (azure with three golden hawks' bells), and panelling gilded or painted with the same motif which gave the room its name of the 'Cabinet aux Grelots'.

It was Paul Ardier, owner of Beauregard in the 17th century, who commissioned the gallery of 363 portraits of French kings, queens, ministers and courtesans; from the first Valois, Charles V, to King Louis XIII. Three centuries of history are illustrated through their most important personalities. The ceiling beams of this remarkable gallery are garlanded with arabesques painted by the artist Jean Mosnier, and the floor is paved with Delft ceramic tiles depicting an army drawn up in battle order.

Opening dates and times
3 Feb-30 Mar and 8 Oct-31 Dec, daily 9.30–12 and 2–5.
31 Mar-30 Jun and 1 Sep-7 Oct, daily 9.30–12 and 2–6.30.

❹ Blois

The château of Blois, with its complex of buildings dating from the 13th to the 17th centuries, is one of the grandest on the Loire; royal palace for Louis XII, François I and Henri III, it also served as a luxurious prison for Marie de' Medici and later for Gaston d'Orléans, under Louis XIII.

All that remains of the former château of the 13th-century Counts of Blois is the principal room divided into two galleries beneath a panelled double-barrel vault supported on seven columns.

The 15th-century 'Charles d'Orléans' gallery, built of brick and stone, has simple lines and elegant proportions. At ground-floor level its flattened arches rest on octagonal pillars, and the upper storey, decorated with two cable mouldings, has casements framed by stone chains beneath gable roofs.

In the Louis XII wing (1498–1503) the polychrome effect of brick and stone combines with a mixture of Flamboyant proportions and Italian-type motifs. Although the stone-masons were French, the sculptors were Italian: they inserted windows of carved stone, pierced balustrades, high dormer windows with pinnacles and gables, finials and armorial bearings; the columns supporting the arches of the lower gallery are decorated with lozenges of fleurs-de-lys and flecked with ermines or arabesques. The grand main porch beneath its Flamboyant pediment frames an equestrian statue of Louis XII with his personal emblem: a porcupine.

The François I wing (1515–1524) contrasts with all this in the whiteness of its tufa stone: foreign influence predominates here. The exterior face, known as 'les Loges', is the earliest French attempt at regular bays, based on Bramante's Roman original; but the French preference for asymmetry is apparent here in the turrets projecting from the façade and in the gargoyles. A carved band half way up the façade bears the alternating initial letter and emblem of François I: an F and a salamander.

But the most notable feature of the building is the open-work staircase tower on the inner façade 'carved out like a Chinese ivory figure' according to Balzac, and ornamented with foliage and classical medallions, with statues in niches, its pierced flights of stairs again carved with the letter F and salamanders. It leads to a lacy stone balustrade extending the full length of the façade.

The Gaston d'Orléans wing, built by François Mansart between 1635 and 1638, is striking in the purity of its style and wholly classical strictness. Inside it has a stairwell topped by a dome and embellished with ornate carved emblems.

Opening dates and times
2 Jan-14 Mar and 2 Nov-31 Dec, daily 9.30–11.45 and 2–4.45.
1 Oct-1 Nov, daily 9.30–12 and 2–6.
15 Mar-30 Sep, daily 9–6.

❺ Chambord

Chambord, lying at the centre of its 5,500-hectare park, is the largest of the Loire châteaux. Construction continued from 1519 until 1552, mostly during the reign of François I, and the scale of the building, with its 128-metre façade, 440 rooms and 74 staircases, was symbolic of French power and wealth.

This 'hunting lodge', designed on the principles of a château set in flat open country, consists of a vast rectangular *enceinte* surrounded by embankments and terraces, and divided into sections by round towers. The main body of the château, flanked by four corner towers, is the '*donjon*' or keep, which is also the most interesting element from the aesthetic point of view. Here the simplicity of the façade up to the parapet walk acts as a foundation for the profusion of chimneys, dormer windows, spires, turrets and stairwells which appear as a luxuriant forest of stone, abounding with carvings and ornamentation. This Italianate upper section, attributed to Leonardo da Vinci and designed to be seen from a distance, is emphasized by the addition of lozenges and circles of slate set in the white stone.

Inside the château the famous double spiral of the richly carved staircase circles upwards, its design – superimposing two endless coils – producing a magical visual effect and playing games with the laws of perspective. Two people who each take one of the spirals are always visible to each other and expect to meet at any moment without ever being able to do so. François I's emblems can be seen from the staircase, carved on the coffered vaults of the antechambers.

Abandoned by royalty and threatened with ruin, Chambord was restored in 1640 by Louis XIII's brother Gaston d'Orléans, who was as passionate about architecture as he was devoted to intrigue. Thirty years later Molière staged his *Bourgeois Gentilhomme* here, with music by Lully, in the presence of Louis XIV and his Court.

Opening dates and times
2 Jan-31 Mar and 1 Oct-31 Dec, daily 9.30–11.45 and 2–4.45.
1 Apr-30 Jun and 1-30 Sep, daily 9.30–11.45 and 2–5.45.
1 Jul-31 Aug, daily 9.30–6.45.

❻ Chaumont-sur-Loire

Demolished on the order of Louis XI in 1466 and rebuilt between 1472 and 1511 by the lords of Amboise, this château has two contrasting aspects.

From the west, the view is of a strong wall, menacing and proud, surmounted by a parapet walk with battlements, crenellations and arrow-slits, plain and unadorned.

The south-east side is elegantly ornamented and surrounded with a strip of decorative carving, with alternating motifs of the initials of Charles of Amboise and a fiery mountain, symbol of Chaumont (*chauds monts*, hot mountains).

The carved pediment over the entrance bears the initials of Louis XII and Anne of Brittany on a background of fleurs-de-lys and ermine, while the towers on each side of the gate display the armorial bearings of Charles and Georges d'Amboise.

Forced on the beautiful Diane de Poitiers as a country retreat, the château displays her signs and emblems carved between the machicolations of the rampart walk: interlaced Ds, bows and quivers, and deltas (the Greek letter D) with three crescents.

Two hundred and fifty years later another distinguished exile, Madame de Staël, was banished from Paris by Napoleon and lived here for six months; among other opponents of Napoleon she received here the writer Benjamin Constant and Madame de Recamier.

In 1875 the château was acquired by the future bride of the Prince de Broglie and benefited greatly from the wealthy art-lover's contributions: to her we owe the elegant wellhead with statuettes in the inner courtyard, and Salerno ceramic tiles in the council chamber which the Prince de Broglie imported from Italy.

Opening dates and times
2 Jan-31 Mar and 1 Oct-31 Dec, daily 9.15–11.35 and 1.45–3.50.
1 Apr-30 Jun and 1-30 Sep, daily 9.15–11.35 and 1.45–5.35.
1 Jul-31 Aug, daily 9–6.

❼ Chenonceau

Thomas Bohier, the financial administrator, bought the château of Chenonceau on 8 February 1513. He renovated the Tour de Marques, the only part he retained, in the current fashion, letting in more light and adding dormer windows surrounded with carved Renaissance decoration.

Between 1515 and 1522 he built his own dwelling on the piles of a former mill standing in the River Cher; the result is a square Renaissance pavilion flanked by four small corner turrets with conical roofs, and two projecting wings framing a terrace on one side.

CHENONCEAU CHATEAU

In the middle of the 16th century Henri II gave the château to his mistress Diane de Poitiers, who commissioned the architect Philibert Delorme to build a bridge out from the château across the river. Italian-style flower-beds were designed by Pacello da Mercoliano and laid out beside the Tour de Marques. After passing into the hands of Catherine de' Medici the château continued to expand: Philibert Delorme, still in fashion with the Court, built a richly ornamented two-storey gallery on the bridge, and Bernard Palissy prepared designs for the 'Garden of Delights', later completed by Le Nôtre in the 17th century.

Inside, visitors can see the guardroom, floored with Italian majolica tiles and hung with 16th-century Flemish tapestries; the coffered ceiling and mantelpiece signed by Jean Goujon in Diane de Poitiers' bedroom; Catherine de' Medici's green room, with a striking Aubusson tapestry; the carved oak ceiling in the library; the François I hall and the salon, both with paintings by Primaticcio, Van Loo, Rubens and Nattier; and the staircase with its straight flights beneath a coffered ceiling. Finally, a waxwork museum illustrates great historical moments in Chenonceau's past.
Opening dates and times
1-15 Mar 9–6.
16 Mar-15 Sep 9–7.
16-30 Sep 9–6.30.
1-31 Oct 9–6.
1-15 Nov 9–5.
16 Nov-15 Feb 9–4.30.
16-28 Feb 9–5.30.

❽ Cheverny

The pure classical style of Cheverny, begun in 1634 by Henri Hurault, distinguishes it from other Loire châteaux; its emphasis on horizontal design contrasts with the more markedly vertical lines of French Renaissance architecture.

Consisting of a central rectangular main section with a shallow projecting centre bay, it is marked by the irregular roof which is nonetheless symmetrically balanced; at each end is an enormous four-sectioned dome on a square base, with a lantern at the top. These form the frame for three sloping roof sections, that of the stairwell, in the middle, being set at right-angles between the other two.

The large rectangular stone slabs add to the horizontal lines of the building, and make up a chequer-board on the façades. On the entrance side, further emphasizing the same lines, twelve niches in a row along the first floor level between the windows contain busts of Roman emperors.

The interior decoration reveals the same homogeneous style: two Louis XIV commodes, one of Chinese lacquer, in the great and small salons; a regulator timepiece (forerunner of the calendar clock) decorated with tooled Calfieri bronzes; and a substantial collection of paintings – Titian, the school of Raphael, François Clouet, and the famous landscape artist Hubert Robert, are all represented here.

A majestic staircase embellished with fruit and symbols of warfare leads to the King's chamber with its series of French tapestries depicting the wanderings of Odysseus, and a fresco of the Perseus myth on the ceiling, painted by Jean Mosnier. It was Mosnier too who created the thirty-four panels of the epic of Don Quixote in the dining room, where the walls are covered with Cordoba leather stamped with the Hurault coat of arms.
Opening dates and times
1-31 Mar 9.30–12 and 2.15–5.30.
1 Apr-31 May 9.15–12 and 2.15–6.30.
1 Jun-15 Sep 9.15–6.45.
16-30 Sep 9.30–12 and 2.15–6.
1-31 Oct 9.30–12 and 2.15–6.45.
1 Nov-28 Feb 9.30–12 and 2.15–5.

❾ La Ferté-Saint-Aubin

For five hundred years a manor house stood on the site of the present-day château, guarding the 'Cosson crossing'.

This vast group of buildings, consisting of a large brick and stone château and its outbuildings, was built by Henri de Sennecterre – followed by his son – during the first half of the 17th century. Its classical inspiration is apparent in the quadripartite domes on top of the square pavilions on either side of the bridge, and the simple ornamentation enhanced by polychromatic design.

From the kitchens to the attics, models in period dress illustrate château life during its different periods.
Opening dates and times
16 Mar-11 Nov, daily 10–6.

❿ Fontevraud-l'Abbaye

Founded in 1099, Fontevraud Abbey enjoyed great power and fame until the French Revolution in 1789. A veritable city created on a completely new site, it included five convents or monasteries under the sole authority of an abbess, who enjoyed considerable power and in many cases was linked by blood or intrigue with the royal family.

FONTEVRAUD ABBEY

The abbey, which enjoyed the protection of the nobility and the Court, provided refuge for repudiated queens, and for well-born young girls without a husband or wishing to complete their education.

Among its most celebrated abbesses were Marie de Bretagne in the 15th century, Louise de Bourbon in the 16th century, and Gabrielle de Rochechouart de Mortemart, sister of Madame de Montespan, in the 17th century. This learned woman added great cultural prestige to the abbey, sustaining an extensive philosophical and literary correspondence with the leading personalities of her day.

The abbey church, known as 'Le Grand Moustier', contains the tombs and effigies of the English Plantagenet King Henry II, his wife Eleanor of Aquitaine, and their son Richard the Lionheart. Carved out of tufa, these impressive examples of 12th-century monumental sculpture create an atmosphere of intense serenity by the great and undramatized simplicity of their sculptural design. Another effigy worthy of mention, that of the 13th-century Isabelle d'Angoulême – widow of King John – is made of wood. The kitchen known as the 'Tour d'Evrault' in the Ste-Marie cloister is an archi-

tectural curiosity with its scalloped roof layout and complex octangular design.
Opening dates and times
1 Apr-16 Sep, daily 9–7.
17 Sep-31 Mar, daily 9.30–12 and 2–5.

⓫ Gien
The château of Gien was built in 1484 by Anne de Beaujeu, the eldest daughter of Louis XI. It replaced an earlier fortress used in 1429 by Joan of Arc, to whom the church attached to the château is dedicated.

Consisting of two main sections set at right-angles, the château has a round tower and a square tower on the side facing the river; on the inner façade the staircase and towers have cut-off angles at their base, topped with pointed roofs, either cone-shaped or in flat sections.

The château's aesthetic attraction lies in the mixed colours of its design: the red and black bricks forming lozenges, chequer-board and herringbone patterns are set between the windows of white stone, and the slate roofs add their own contrasting shade.

Since 1952 the château has been the home of the International Museum of Hunting. Pictures, tapestries, engravings, trophies, statues, pottery, and a collection of weapons illustrate the martial skills which were the favourite royal pastime in times of peace.

The great hall with its ceiling vault, shaped like an upturned keel, is devoted to the 18th-century artist François Desporte, famous for his portrayal of animals; nearly 100 of his paintings are on view.

Among the weapons collected here are a gun bearing a portrait of Louis XIV and the double-barrelled flintlocks of Napoleon and his general Cambronne. The tapestries include a remarkable 17th-century Brussels representation of hawking.
Opening dates and times
1 Mar-30 Apr and 1 Oct-31 Dec, daily except Mon 10–12 and 2–5.
1-31 May, weekdays 10–12 and 2–5, Sat and Sun 9.30–6.30.

⓬ Langeais
In the 10th century Langeais was an impressive stronghold belonging to the redoubtable Count of Anjou, known as the Black Falcon – 'Foulques Nerra' – for his ferocity in war, and whose ambition was matched only by his cruelty.

Rebuilt between 1451 and 1469 by Louis XI, the château is a perfect illustration of contemporary military architecture, and its imposing and sombre appearance is in keeping with the austere power of its king.

All the distinctive features of its construction relate to military use: the 130-metre parapet walk is surmounted by enclosed towers, there is a defensive embankment, crenellations form a firing vantage-point, a drawbridge between two towers shields the entrance. Once inside the inner courtyard the look of the château is less menacing, and although the simplicity of the decoration is a constant reminder of the military purpose of the building, its Renaissance elegance is expressed in the five storeys of window bays, the mullions, the decorated dormer windows, and the turrets with angled cut-off sections.

It was here that Louis XI's son Charles VIII married Anne of Brittany in 1491, bringing to an end the hostility between France and Brittany which had been the original reason for building the castle – a peaceful fate for a military building, the setting for a highly diplomatic union.

Inside, visitors can admire the enormous chimneypieces, a relief carving of the château and its men-at-arms ready for battle, and patterned tiling. Moving from room to room, you can see the credence-tables, chests, canopied beds, and Flemish, Aubusson and Tours tapestries, the furnishings for a royal household of the 15th century.
Opening dates and times
31 Nov-14 Mar, daily except Mon 9–12 and 2–5.
15 Mar-2 Nov, daily 9–6.30.

⓭ Loches
Built on a rocky plateau, the château of Loches was an important fortress from the 6th to the 12th centuries, as indicated by the enormous square keep dating from the 11th century. Loches was used as a prison from the 13th to the 15th centuries, when the round corner tower was added, together with the building known as 'Le Martelet', and the drawbridge. A royal establishment in the 15th and 16th centuries, Agnès Sorel made her home here, and Louis XI and François I were both visitors for brief periods.

The fortress is approached through the 13th-century royal gate, flanked by two massive towers; inside, the Romanesque church of St-Ours is remarkable for its carved triple-arched porch and its nave beneath two hollow pyramids.

The tower has an alabaster effigy of the 'Dame de Beauté', lying on a black marble plinth, with two leaning angels at her head and two lambs intertwined at her feet.

The royal lodge next to the tower includes a 14th-century section with military-style rooms where Charles VII first met Joan of Arc in 1429. The 15th-century part of the building was the domestic dwelling, decorated with mullion windows and with elaborate dormer windows in the attics surrounded by stone dogs. The chapel displays the arms of Anne of Brittany.

Visitors can also see the dark maze of prison cells in the 'Martelet', cut out of the rock itself, and still showing the inscriptions carved by famous inmates, including the Duke of Milan, Ludovic Sforza . . . or they can dally in front of Fouquet's charming portrait of Agnès Sorel.
Opening dates and times
1 Feb-14 Mar and 1 Oct-30 Nov, daily except Wed 9–12 and 2–5.
15 Mar-30 Jun and 1-30 Nov, daily 9–12 and 2–6.
1 Jul-31 Aug, daily 9–6.

⓮ Meillant
Begun at the end of the 14th century by Charles I and finished between 1501 and 1511 by Charles II of Amboise, the château of Meillant is undoubtedly one of the grandest

examples of Flamboyant Gothic in the Loire Valley.

The château's setting, in the midst of a forest surrounded by marshland, demanded no great defensive construction, and elegance of style took first priority.

Under the direction of the Italian architect Fra Giocondo a chapel was added and the famous hexagonal tower, known as the 'Tour du Lion', was built. Its luxuriant ornamentation stands out sharply against the almost bare walls of the façade. Each of its ribs is festooned with a twisted colonnette, and it is completely covered with arcaded panels and varied motifs: emblems of Chaumont and Charles d'Amboise (interlaced Cs and fiery mountains), and figurines of armed men. More Italianate, and thus more Renaissance in style, the top of the tower has semi-circular arcading and is topped by a lantern-dome.

The dormer windows in the roof have lacy stone ridges beneath chimneys which are themselves clad with false dormers and false guard rails.

Inside the château, the 200-square-metre grand salon has a magnificent Renaissance chimneypiece, with a gallery above designed for musicians. The bedroom of the Cardinal d'Amboise is furnished entirely in the 17th-century Flemish style.

Opening dates and times
1 Feb-15 Dec, daily 9–11.30 and 2–6.30.

⓯ Ménars
The central section of the 1650 building is Classical in style, the main part of which is rendered in plaster with decorative chains of brick standing out in contrast. Roofed with slate there is a slightly projecting pavilion at each end. A large, formally planted terrace with lime trees overlooks the Loire, with lawn, canal and ornamental water below making up the gardens which date from 1675.

Bought by Madame de Pompadour in 1760, the château was extended by two wings and decorative carved wooden panelling added to the rooms. Her brother, the Marquis de Marigny, worked on improvements to the garden between 1765 and 1780; statues and ornamental basins, orangerie and rotunda. Soufflot's grotto, an English-style garden and a Temple of Love remain today as part of its delights.

This château is not open to the public.

⓰ Poncé-sur-le-Loir
Built in the 16th century, this Renaissance château consists of a tall central section containing the staircase, flanked by two wings. The bays of casement windows framed within superimposed pilasters and a double moulded string-course between the storeys belong to the Loire region in style, while the dormer pediments are in the Ile-de-France tradition. The entrance on the north side of the building is on the first floor, level with a terrace resting on Roman-style arches.

The château's most successful architectural element is the Renaissance staircase with its six straight flights, of which the first three spans lie beneath flat vaulting and the next two under rounded vaults. They are decorated with panels with various motifs such as rosettes, horns of plenty, armorial bearings, cherubs, pagan gods, salamanders, stags, dormice, foliage etc.

The garden has an attractive hornbeam maze.

Opening dates and times
1 Apr-30 Sep, daily 10–12 and 2–6.
Sun and official holidays, 2–6.

⓱ Saumur
Standing on a rock overlooking the valley, the château at Saumur was built at the end of the 14th century by Louis I of Anjou, brother of Charles V. It was immortalized in all its splendour when the Flemish artist Pol de Limbourg was commissioned by the Duke Jean de Berry, a great collector of miniature paintings, to create his 'Book of Hours' in the 15th century.

The pictures of *Les Très Riches Heures du Duc de Berry*, preserved at Chantilly and widely reproduced, enable us to see and appreciate the management of the château in the days of its glory: the richness and delicacy of the superstructure combine with the enduring strength of the sober walls below; luxuriant ornamentation adorns the crenellation with great carved fleurs-de-lys, and gilded weathervanes gleam on the little turrets.

SAUMUR CHATEAU

Fortified in about 1590 by its governor, Duplessis-Mornay, the château is surrounded by a star-shaped enclosure. The façades are decorated with bays with moulded arcading beneath niches, and turrets with pointed roofs and cut-off corners. In the 18th century the north-west wing was demolished to make room for a terrace with a view out over the River Loire and the town. The elegant inner court is surrounded by an Italianate arcaded gallery.

The Museum of Decorative Art inside the château displays enamels, wood-carvings and alabaster sculpture, a remarkable array of 16th, 17th and 18th-century furniture and tapestries, and an important collection of ceramics, pottery and porcelain consisting of 1,300 items from every part of France. The exhibition halls are hung with magnificent period tapestries.

Opening dates and times
1 Apr-15 Jun, daily 9–11.30 and 2–6.
15 Jun-15 Sep, daily 9–6.30.

⑱ Sully-sur-Loire

Standing above the Loire and surrounded by immense moats on all sides, Sully-sur-Loire gives the impression of being built on the water.

The medieval style old château, or keep, makes up the north wing; consisting of a rectangular donjon with four round towers at the corners and high curtain walls beneath a parapet walk, it was built by the La Trémoille family in the 15th century. In 1430 Joan of Arc was the unwilling guest of George de La Trémoille, Charles VII's favourite and councillor.

The Béthune Tower and, at right angles to it, the wing known as the 'Sully lodge', were added in the 17th century, named after their builder and the château's owner at the time, Maximilien de Béthune. Duke of Sully and minister to Henri IV, he retired to the château in 1611, the year of his disgrace. Sully's study is in this part of the building, and also the king's bedroom with its *trompe-l'oeil* panelling and two 17th-century tapestries. The guardroom on the ground floor of the old château, used each year for a famous music festival, has vast ornamental stone fireplaces.

A gallery of portraits of the Béthune seigneurs hangs in the grand reception room on the first floor, which has a superb Gothic fireplace with a classical-style painting above it. The double span chapel next to it, with ogive vaulting, contains a picture of Sully and his wife at prayer.

The wooden roof-beams in the form of an upturned keel in the remarkable great salon on the upper floor derive both strength and lightness from their Y-shaped design.

Opening dates and times
1-31 Mar and 1-30 Nov, daily 10–11.45 and 2–4.45.
1-30 Apr and 1-31 Oct, daily 10–11.45 and 2–5.45.
1 May-30 Oct, daily 9–11.45 and 2–5.45.

⑲ Talcy

This fortified house was built in the 15th century, with a main keep and square donjon. In its courtyard a two-storey gallery, copied from the gallery of the Charles d'Orléans wing at Blois, has open flattened arches at ground level, supported on octagonal columns. It is enclosed at the upper level, its casements decorated with moulded string-courses beneath crocketed gables at roof level.

The wealthy Bernard Salviati, from Florence, bought Talcy in 1517 and added the machicolated rampart walk and the stair tower with its turret adjoining the donjon. Some of the most famous lines in French 16th-century literature were inspired here: 183 of the poet Ronsard's love sonnets are dedicated to Salviati's daughter Cassandra, and his grand-daughter Diane inspired the love of Agrippa d'Aubigné.

In 1562 Catherine de' Medici brought Catholics and Protestants together at Talcy, in a vain attempt at reconciliation.

Opening dates and times
2 Jan-31 Mar and 1 Oct-31 Dec, daily except Tues 10–11.15 and 2–4.30.
1-30 Apr, daily except Tues 9.30–11.15 and 2–6.

TALCY CHATEAU

2 May-30 Jun and 1-30 Sep, daily 9.30–11.15 and 2–6.
1 Jul-31 Aug, daily from 9.30–6.

⑳ Ussé

Standing on the banks of the River Indre and on the edge of the forest of Chinon, Ussé and its unorthodox beauty are said to have been the inspiration for 'The Sleeping Beauty' fairy tale by Charles Perrault. Its various styles – Gothic, Flamboyant, Renaissance and Classical – illustrate several centuries of architectural history.

The exterior façades flanked with great machicolated towers, the parapet walk, and the donjon, date from the days of the lords of Bueil in the 15th century; facing the courtyard, the western wing, built by the d'Espinay family in the 16th century, displays a purely Renaissance style in its pillars and high dormers.

The 17th century brought fresh modifications along with a change of owner; the north wing was removed, opening the château towards the valley, classical bays were added to the south wing, and ornamental terraces of orange trees, attributed to Vauban, sloped down to the River Indre.

The cedars at the entrance have a romantic history: they were a gift from Chateaubriand in the 19th century on one of his visits to his mistress, the Duchesse de Duras.

The interior of the château retains its inheritance from all these periods, and its furnishings are a history of the evolution of the decorative arts; they include a 16th-century Italian cabinet which is remarkable for the rich delicacy of its marquetry of ebony inlaid with ivory and mother-of-pearl.

The Gothic-style chapel, with its Italianate ornamentation, was consecrated in 1583; it is a

particularly pure example of the early French Renaissance – shells garlanded with foliage in the porch, statuettes set in wall medallions and carved pews.
Opening dates and times
15 Mar-14 Apr, daily 9–12 and 2–6.
15 Apr-30 Sep, daily 9–12 and 2–7.
1 Oct-1 Nov, daily 10–12 and 2–6.

㉑ La Verrerie
Set in the forest of Ivoy beside a pool of the River Nère, the château of La Verrerie belonged for two hundred years to the Stuarts: Charles VII offered the property to the Constable Jean Stuart de Darnley, second son of the King of Scotland, in 1423.

Béraud Stuart, his son, built a chapel facing the pool and a keep with a porch flanked by corbelled towers. A hexagonal tower dominates the surrounding enclosure.

Home from his Italian campaigns, his son-in-law Robert Stuart added Italian elegance to the château. Between 1515 and 1525 he replaced the outer wall by a further wing, with an open loggia at ground level, with basket-handle arches resting on elegant and richly carved columns bearing the arms of the Stuarts and spandrels encrusted with medallions.

Robert Stuart also commissioned the painting of frescoes on the chapel walls and medallions on the vaulting, including portraits of Charles VII and Jean Stuart.

In the 17th century Louis XIV took back the château and gave it to Louise de Kéroualle, former mistress of Charles II of England, who for thirty years continued to improve the property.

In 1842 the château was sold to Léonce de Vogue, a noble at the court of Charles X, who was responsible for the new keep behind the 16th-century wing, in a revival of the Flamboyant style.
Opening dates and times
15 Feb-15 Nov, daily 10–12 and 2–7.

㉒ Villandry
Villandry was built in the middle of the 16th century by Jean Le Breton, secretary to François I. It is both the last of the great Renaissance châteaux to be built in the Loire Valley and the first sign of the architectural spirit of the Ile-de-France, an influence visible in the square pavilions which here replace the traditional round corner towers.

Raised above its terrace on the banks of the River Cher, it displays arcaded Italianate galleries on richly decorated columns at ground level, and gardens on three successive levels of terracing designed in the 16th century by Androuet Du Cerceau – landscape architect to the Court – and reconstructed by Dr Joachim Carvallo, who acquired Villandry in 1906.

The château contains a remarkable collection of Spanish paintings, including works by Velasquez, El Greco, Morales, Ribera, Zurbaran and Goya, and another Spanish feature, a Toledo carved and painted ceiling dating from the 18th century.

Regarded as being among the 300 finest gardens in France, the Villandry château park includes a water garden where ingeniously designed pools, fountains, canals, bridges and waterfalls give a refreshing effect in their setting of greenery; and a 'Garden of Love', laid out in a dramatic mosaic of flowerbeds, to represent the four 'acts' in the eternal tragi-comedy of love – seduction, passion, infidelity, vengeance.

And finally the unique ornamental vegetable garden, spread across a hectare of land, consists of nine beds arranged in geometrical patterns and punctuated with fruit trees, rose bushes and jasmine-covered arches.
Opening dates and times
(Château) 15 Mar-11 Sep, daily 9–6
(Gardens) 1 Jun-31 Aug, daily 8.45–8.
16 Mar-31 May and 1-30 Sep, daily 8.45–7.
1 Jan-15 Mar and 1 Oct-31 Dec, daily 9–6.15.

The following is a glossary of architectural periods and terms used in this article:

Romanesque: 10th–12th centuries
Gothic: 12th–15th centuries (Flamboyant Gothic – 15th century)
Renaissance: 15th–16th centuries
Classical: 17th–18th centuries
Arabesque: Intricate surface decoration combining geometrical patterns and flowing lines.
Arcading: A series of arches carried on columns.
Corbel: A projecting block, usually stone, supporting a beam or other horizontal weight.
Crenellations: Also known as a battlement – a low wall with alternating recesses and raised sections.
Crocket: Decorative feature, projecting at regular intervals from the corners of spires, carved in leaf shapes.
Enceinte: Main enclosure of a fortress, surrounded by a wall or ditch.
Finial: Formal ornament on top of a canopy, gable, pinnacle, etc.
Lantern: A polygonal or circular turret with windows all round, on top of a room, dome or roof.
Loggia: A gallery open on one or more sides.
Machicolation: Built on the outside of castle towers and walls, a parapet projecting on brackets, with openings in the floor to drop molten lead, etc.
Mullion: An upright post dividing the light in a window.
Pediment: A low-pitched gable above a portico and a similar feature above doors, windows, etc.
Pilaster: Masonry support or column projecting from a wall.
String-course: A continuous raised horizontal band or course of bricks on an exterior wall, usually moulded.
Trompe-l'oeil: Painting or decoration giving a convincing illusion of reality.
Tufa: Commonly used building stone, formed from volcanic dust, grey and porous.

FOOD AND WINE

THE 'GARDEN OF FRANCE'

The Loire region's gastronomy has no very marked or exclusive characteristics, indeed its individuality is based on its diversity – the natural result of the great variety and abundance of its produce.

Loire cooking is both simple and sophisticated: the simplicity is derived from its peasant traditions, which for over two hundred years were counterbalanced by the refinements of the 'gilded nobility' and the royal courts. As with its architecture and châteaux, the result is a skilful blend of plainness and richness.

If it is true, as great writers have suggested, that a nation's culture is the expression of its soul, it is impossible to know the Loire Valley thoroughly without lingering over its food and its wines.

The Berry

It was Jacques Coeur, 1395–1456, the great traveller and merchant and royal Treasurer, who is said to have introduced 'Turkish chickens', or turkeys, which are a speciality of this region, roasted on a spit as in olden times. The ships of this Marco Polo of Bourges also imported the eastern spices which became an essential ingredient of another Bourges speciality, its gingerbread.

Classics among the robust and savoury local soups are the rich *soupe aux tartouffes* (with potatoes), and onion soup made with wine.

Farming here traditionally means livestock rearing, and Berry has a reputation for producing the best sheep in France: the local breed, famous for its flavour, even appears on heraldic arms; and 'seven hour' braised leg of lamb is the most characteristic dish. Since this is a region of game, red and grey partridge, hare, corncrake, quail and woodcock also appear on the menu. Poultry are cooked on the spit or *en barbouille*, in a sauce made with wine and blood. Fish, particularly trout and carp, are prepared in red wine; and mushrooms such as cepes, chanterelles, St George's and field mushrooms add their flavour to meat and sauces.

Among the many local goat cheeses, the best known is the Crottin de Chavignol; one of the creamiest is the cut-off pyramid shape of the Valençay.

Sweet dishes in the rural tradition are fairly substantial; apple *gouerons*, fritters and vast pancakes. *Lichouneries* are the most delicate of confectionery, and there are the *croquets* or almond biscuits of Charost and Sancerre, *forestines* from Bourges, and the wild-rose jam known as *gargaillou*.

AOC white wines

'AOC' = *Appellation d'Origine Contrôlée*, i.e. wines of higher quality, guaranteed to derive from a particular locality:

Sancerre: white wines from the marl soils are robust and gain their bouquet after a few months in the bottle, while those from chalky soils are light and fruity, excellent for drinking *en primeur*, that is, very young. Interesting rosés, reds produced as in Burgundy.

GRAPES IN THE WINEPRESS

FOOD AND WINE

PREPARATION OF TERRINES AND PATES

Menetou-Salon: fresh, fruity and quite substantial, with an earthy taste.
Quincy: a very dry white wine, fresh and without acidity.
Reuilly: very similar to Quincy.
Pouilly-sur-Loire: a young wine, acidic and light, delicate, open, with a hazelnut taste.
Pouilly-Fumé: well-fruited, robust but not hard, with notes of musk and spice.

VDQS wines
VDQS = *Vins Délimité de Qualité Supérieure* i.e. claiming to be rather better than the 'ordinary' *du pays* country wines:
Valençay and the *vin gris* from Châteaumeillant.

Spirits
Cherry brandy from Le Blanc, marc.

Orléanais and Blésois regions
Pâtés made from local game in each district were already famous in medieval times; thrushes in Gien, larks in Blois and Pithiviers, plover and rabbit in Beaugency, venison and hare in Anet and Chartres. Sologne is the supreme source of abundant game for a variety of recipes which have become classics: partridge *à la coque* (stuffed with foie gras), young rabbit *à la solognotte*, wild duck with apple fritters, pheasant *en barbouille*, *cuissot* of wild boar (marinated and roasted), haunch of venison, and hare *à la beauceronne*.

The local farm-bred poultry, as famous as that of Bresse, is prepared with equal skill and diversity: chicken *à la crème* or *sauté* at Bellegarde, or as *coq au vin* (with *vin gris*) *meunier*, rabbit in red wine at Gien and Orléans, spatchcocked pigeon, goose with apples, roast turkey or duck, grilled or sautéed capon.

And you will find all the traditional sorts of charcuterie: pâté, potted mince, smoked pork and sausage, and a distinctive black pudding made from wild boar. Pork also appears as a *carbonade* in a casserole, the local speciality; or there is simmered leg of lamb from Orléans, aitchbone of beef *à la beauceronne*, or braised and larded veal with orange from Blois.

The many local fish dishes should not be ignored either: *quenelles* of pike poached in wine, carp, eels from the River Cisse, trout from the Loir and the Boulon.

Among sweets and desserts the crystallized plums from Blois, dating from the Renaissance and known as *pistoles*, are the best known. Other fruit conserves are apricot cheese, Orléans *cotignac* (quince marmalade), and Beaugency fruit cheeses.

Pithiviers almond cake and the Tatin sisters' 'upside-down' apple or pear tart barely need a mention for their fame contributes to the national reputation for gastronomic success.

Finally, the spread of good fare is completed with honey from the Gâtinais, pralines from Montargis, and chocolates from Blois.

AOC wines
Touraine-Mesland: fresh and fruity rosé wines; delicate white wines full of fruit and bouquet; full-bodied red wines.

VDQS wines
From Orléans: *Auvernat* and *Gris-Meunier Orléanais*, *Côtes de Gien*.
From Blois: *Coteaux-du-Vendômois*, *Cheverny*.

Spirits
Around Orléans: cherry, pear or hazelnut brandy, strawberry liqueur, marc.
Around Blois: strawberry liqueur, marc, brandy.

The Touraine

The widely varied gastronomy of this region reflects the variety and abundance of local produce.

Among the many fish of the Loire and its tributaries are shad from the Loire itself, prepared either with mushrooms or marinated with diced bacon, pike from the Cher, and carp from the Indre, all cooked with elegance and simplicity.

Game and poultry appear in stews or fricassees, such as the *géline de Touraine* (chicken), while shoulder of mutton may be stuffed, and goat prepared in the same way as a leg of lamb. Pork is used in many ways, including the fillet cooked with prunes, or as charcuterie – Tours and Vouvray are famous for their *andouilles* and *rillettes* (sausages and pâté). Country *rillettes* are less delicate but richer, made to an older recipe.

The Loire valley is the uncontested kingdom of asparagus, while the *argouanes des prairies* (field mushrooms) make an outstanding soup. Other fruit and vegetable specialities include green walnuts in verjuice – unripe walnuts macerated in juice from unripe grapes – to eat with salads.

It was Rabelais who created the fame of *fouace* or gridle cakes in his writings, and they are still the most famous of Touraine desserts, but others worth seeking out are *cordées* or plaited milk-bread, *russeroles* – a type of fritter, and a frumenty of wheat mixed with almond milk.

AOC wines

Chinon: red and rosé wines, violet-scented, fruity with a taste of wild strawberries, delicate, soft and sweet; they age well.

Bourgueil and **St-Nicolas-de-Bourgueil**: sinewy and powerful, quite dry, fruity with a raspberry note and violet-scented. They mellow with age and should be drunk after four or five years.

Vouvray: (whites). Vouvray 'nature' (a still wine) is sappy and fruity, with plenty of bouquet, a hint of acacia in its scent and a note of quince in its taste. Sparkling or semi-sparkling versions are also available.

Montlouis: (whites). Similar to Vouvray in taste, light and delicate, with a good bouquet, sometimes offering a gun-flint flavour or even its own particular touch of hazelnut; it may also be sparkling.

Touraine-Azay-le-Rideau: dry or sweet white wines, fresh-tasting and always fruity.

Touraine-Amboise: fine fruity white wines with good bouquet, and full-bodied reds.

Spirits

Brandy made from William pears or prunes, marc.

Anjou

The Loire and its tributaries are unfailing in their supply of fish – gudgeon, pike, eel, even salmon, all ingredients of Anjou's gastronomy. Eels alone are the main element of three specialities – *bouilleture*, a type of fish-stew with red wine; *roulade* with mushrooms, onions and prunes; and pâté. Tench and bream are stuffed with sorrel.

Local charcuterie here too takes on many varied and tasty forms: *rillons*, *rilleaux* and *rillettes*, pork pâtés enriched with local white wine; *Gogues* or flat sausages with leaves of spinach and spiced fat bacon, white pudding, and *andouillettes*, small sausages. *Dâtrée* is a traditional vegetable dish made of cabbage, mashed potatoes and butter.

Pears are the chief local fruit, particularly the well-known Belle Angevine and Comice varieties. Oil from local walnuts is used for salads; and local cheeses to go with the salads are *Chouzé*, *caillebottes à la chardonnette* (curd cheese with cardoons) or *chabis* (goat cheese), *crèmets* (small cream cheeses), and St-Paulin.

A glass of wine goes well with local pâtisserie, sweets or cakes such as *nouzillard*, made from chestnuts, *fouace* from Lerné, *guillaret* (canary-bread) or *fouée*, a yeast-dough pancake.

AOC wines
White wines

Savennières: dry white wines, firm and sinewy, heady, full and elegant. At their best between 5 and 10 years old. Amongst the *grands crus* (fine wines) are the Coulée de Serrant and the Roche-aux-Moines.

Coteaux du Layon: soft and sweet white wines, rounded, fruity, full, substantial, with a delicate bouquet and flavours of apricot or lime-flowers. The sweetest of these wines are Quart-de-Chaumes, Bonnezaux, Domaine-de-Belle-Rive, and Clos-de-la-Roche.

Coteaux de l'Aubance: drier than the Layon white wines, fruity and delicate though robust, with a distinctive local taste. The best commune is Murs-Erigné.

Coteaux de Saumur: light dry white wines, easy drinking but not soft, with a good bouquet. Communes of *grands* and *premiers crus*: Brézé, Montsoreau, Parnay.

MUSHROOM AND HERB FRICASSEE

FOOD AND WINE

Rosé wines
Rosés d'Anjou: fruity, lively, with a pleasingly fresh effect.
Cabernet-d'Anjou and *Cabernet-de-Saumur*: elegant, choice, delicate rosés.

Red wines
Coteaux de Saumur: with an aroma of raspberries, positive, robust and full.
Saumur-Champigny: light and well balanced.
Sparkling wines, white and rosé: *Saumur brut* and *Crémant de Loire*.

Spirits
Anjou brandy and liqueurs.

Matching wine and food
'Good cooking and good wines – heaven on earth' . . . HENRI IV.
White and dry rosé wines: fish, shell-fish, fried fish.
Medium-dry white wines: fish cooked in butter or sauce; charcuterie.
Medium-sweet, sweet, very sweet white wines: sweet fruit dishes, tarts and cakes.
Light red wines: poultry and white meat.
Heavier red wines: red meat.
Full-bodied red wines: game, meat prepared in sauces.
Well-aged and delicate red wines: ideal for mild-flavoured cheeses.
Sparkling or semi-sparkling: dry wines as an aperitif, sweeter wines with desserts.

Acidic flavours do not go well with wine, therefore avoid vinaigrette dressings, highly spiced dishes and citrus fruits.

White and rosé wines should be served chilled, between 6° and 12° Celsius, equivalent to cellar temperature. The best way to chill wine is to plunge it into an ice-bucket; the refrigerator is best avoided since wines served too cold lose bouquet, taste and scent.

Young and light red wines can be drunk chilled, as with white wines; older and heavier red wines should be *chambré*; that is opened two hours before drinking and left to stand in a relatively cool room, with a temperature of between 15° and 17° Celsius and well away from a strong source of heat.

Sparkling wines should be chilled in ice.

GAME CONFITS

The language of wine
A specific vocabulary is devoted to describing the appearance, taste and smell of a wine. While some impressions are purely of taste, other sensations arise from the aroma of the wine within the mouth itself. Indeed, smells are not only absorbed through the nose but also through the mouth where they linger at the back of the throat and pass through the nasal cavities.

There are several dozen words specifically designed to capture the exact taste and effect on the palate. Guaranteed to impress your friends, try some of these next time you are tasting a new wine:

aimable: pleasant, agreeable and nicely balanced
bien en bouche: a rich, well-balanced wine
capiteux: heady; high in alcohol, intoxicating (goes to the head)
charnu: fleshy; fills the mouth well leaving a strong sensation
distingué: distinguished; fine quality wine with its own character
étoffé: full, well constituted; linked also with the rich colour of a wine
exubérant: exuberant, sparkling
franc: honest; natural, clean sound wine without any faults
jeune: young; new wine or wine which has kept its young character
long: long; wine, the taste of which lingers in the mouth with intense aromatic flavour
loyal: faithful; loyal; a natural wine which has been made following all the legal processes, without cheating, and having no hidden vices
mâché: chewy; full-bodied, filling the mouth well
marchand: marketable; wine that has those characteristics required by commercial laws and regulations
nerveux: nervy; vigorous, with good body, a certain acidity, and ageing well
plein: full; well balanced; wine with good body
rassis: settled; well-balanced wine which has finished ageing
solide: solid; well constituted and keeping well
soyeux: silky; wine whose texture recalls the feel of silk
usé: worn-out; wine that is over the hill, too old, having lost its original qualities
velouté: velvety; mellow wine whose texture recalls the feel of velvet
vif: lively; fresh, light wine

LEISURE ACTIVITIES

The following pages cover the prime holiday pursuits in the Loire region. Cycling and riding are perennial favourites, but a spate of course-building in the last ten years reflects the flourishing interest in the game of golf.
The watery landscape of the River Loire and its tributaries invite the angler to pass his time in peaceful leafy corners. The more active can enjoy the walking and motoring itineraries featured, embracing the magnificent château and vineyard scenery.
To further tempt the palate, we suggest tours through wine-producing villages and visits to ancient vineyards, tasting cellars and museums.

LEFT TRADITIONAL SHAD FISHING BOAT

Loisirs Accueil
For holidaymakers who are seeking something different, the Loisirs Accueil organization offers unusual and interesting short break ideas with accommodation arranged in local *gîtes,* hotels or campsites. What is offered varies from one *département* to another, but the main themes of leisure and sporting activities are covered. Thus there are, for example, helicopter or ballooning trips over the châteaux, cycling, riding and canoeing holidays. Another increasingly popular alternative is that of touring in hand-painted, horse-drawn caravans. Slow and leisurely, this type of holiday has immediate and obvious appeal for horse-lovers.
It is worth noting that the majority of these brochures are in French, and where tuition is included in the holiday, this too is likely to be given in French. Your enjoyment of this type of holiday is therefore dependent on having a reasonable command of the French language.
Depending on your area of interest, contact one of the following six offices for further information:

Loisirs Accueil Cher
5 rue Sérancourt, 18000 Bourges
☎ *48.67.01.38*

Loisirs Accueil Eure-et-Loir
19 place des Epars, BP 67, 28000 Chartres
☎ *37.21.37.22*

Loisirs Accueil Indre
Gare routière, 36 rue Bourdillon, 36000 Châteauroux
☎ *54.22.91.20*

Loisirs Accueil Indre-et-Loire
38 rue Augustin-Fresnel, BP 139, 37171 Chambray-lès-Tours
☎ *47.48.37.27*

Loisirs Accueil Loir-et-Cher
11 place du Château, 41000 Blois
☎ *54.78.55.50*

Loisirs Accueil Loiret
3 rue de la Bretonnerie, 45000 Orléans
☎ *38.62.04.88*

SPORTS
Further practical information on the following popular sports and activities can be obtained direct from the addresses given below.
Cycling
Fédération Française de Cyclotourisme
8 rue Jean-Marie Jego, 75013 Paris
Fishing
Conseil Supérieure de la Pêche
134 avenue de Malakoff, 75016 Paris
(local regulations and advice from the Tourist Offices)
Golf
Fédération Française de Golf
69 avenue Victor-Hugo, 75016 Paris
Rambling
Fédération Française de la Randonnée Pédestre (FFRP)
Comité National des Sentiers de Grande Randonnée,
8 avenue Marceau, 75008 Paris
Riding
Association Nationale pour le Tourisme Equestre (ANTE),
15 rue de Bruxelles,
75009 Paris

THE LOIRE

OUTDOOR LEISURE

SOME SPORTING THEMES

CYCLING

A week or two spent on two wheels may well qualify as the 'perfect' French holiday. What could be better than exploring off the beaten track, with picnic lunches bought in quiet villages; or discovering the châteaux amidst long avenues of poplars and willows.

This type of holiday can, of course, be geared to all levels of cyclist and all levels of comfort. Some choose to travel totally self-contained, carrying tent and sleeping bag; others travel to any one of the SNCF stations which operate the *Train + Vélo* bike-hire service, and take their journey on from there; still others book with one of the specialist holiday operators whose prices include flights, bike hire, itineraries, hotel accommodation and daily onward transport of luggage.

Details of how to transport bicycles on the French rail network, and the stations which operate the cycle-hire scheme can be obtained from SNCF French Railways, 179 Piccadilly, London W1V 0BA ☎ 071-493 9731 and from continental rail-appointed travel agents.

Most Tourist Offices in good cycling areas produce excellent short-circuit routes and the Loisirs Accueil organization offers an extensive range of cycling tours throughout the region, often combined with canoeing as well. Loisirs Accueil addresses are on page 27.

FISHING ON THE LOIRE

FISHING

For fishing purposes, French waters are classified into category 1 for salmon and trout and category 2 for all other fish. Fishing waters are either in private ownership or under the control of the State. To fish in private waters, of course, the owner's permission is needed; on State property, an angler, who must be a fully paid up member of an angling association, needs to obtain a permit and pay the annual fishing tax. For category 1 fishing a supplementary tax is levied.

A duly stamped tax card can be obtained from the nearest fishing tackle shop who will also be able to advise about any local regulations, often to be found posted at the *Mairie* or town hall, and will help by recommending the best fishing sites. Information specific to a particular region can be obtained by writing to the relevant *Comité Départemental,* and the Tourist Offices are also particularly helpful. The gazetteer section of this guide includes details of the category of fishing permitted locally.

The Conseil Supérieure de la Pêche (CSP), 134 avenue de Malakoff, 75016 Paris, publishes an excellent pamphlet entitled *Fishing in France*, outlining in great detail the regulations governing the sport, and listing the size limits permitted for certain fish, below which the catch must be thrown back. They also produce a first-class fishing map of France, with a list, in English and French, of the commonest types of fish to be found.

Of particular interest to anglers is the Château de la Bussière which, because of the present owner's large fishing collection, has been nicknamed 'Château des Pêcheurs'. Open daily Mar-Nov, except Tues, it is located 12 km from Briare. Also of interest is the aquarium at Montreuil-Bellay, near Saumur, where more than 400 of the region's fish species are on show. Open daily July-Aug.

Game Fishing (category 1)

In the Loire basin there are fine trout streams in the higher reaches and in the tributaries, and in the upper reaches of the Loiret, between Olivet and Beaugency. The close season is between the third week in September and the first week in March.

Coarse Fishing (category 2)

The Loire and its tributaries – the Cher, Creuse, Sarthe and Loir – teem with coarse fish: barbel, bream, burbot, carp, cat fish, eels, grayling, pike, roach, tench, perch and pollan. The close season for pike is between February and mid-May, otherwise the waters are open throughout

LEISURE ACTIVITIES

THE PARK AT CHAMBORD

the year, from half an hour before dawn to half an hour after dusk.

RIDING

Equestrianism is now the fifth most popular sport in France and the French tourist organization has ensured that riders wishing to have holidays with horses are well catered for.

Where riding centres are located in or close to the resorts in this book, they have been included, but there is also an excellent booklet published by the Association Nationale pour le Tourisme Equestre (ANTE) 15 rue de Bruxelles, 75009 Paris, and any would-be riders in France would do well to obtain a copy (free on request, but enclose £1 postage, from the French Government Tourist Office, 178 Piccadilly, London). It gives a contact address for each *département* in France and hundreds of names and addresses of regional centres. Also worth contacting is the Loisirs Accueil organization (see page 27.)

Types of holiday which you will see mentioned are called *randonnées,* meaning rides, trips or excursions. Thus, a *weekend de Randonnée* takes the rider away from base for one night only, and these are very popular. A *Randonnée* takes the rider away for two to four days and a *Grande Randonnée* can last five days or more.

Accompanied *randonnées* include the cost of the guide, and you will be taken as a group. Tours usually consist of loops so there is no need to retrace the route. Reservations can be made to suit age requirements and some centres specialize in holidays for young riders, offering individual attention.

For those with advanced riding ability it is possible to go out alone or as a private group of friends on itineraries with overnight stays, meals, etc., organized by the centre. Most establishments offer special rates, particularly out of season, for groups of six to eight riders, and it is possible to arrange special 'à la carte' treks outside scheduled itineraries.

Many centres accept holidaymakers who are passing through and just wish to have a *promenade* or an hour's ride, accompanied or not. You can also go out for a half-day trek, while perhaps the most pleasant excursions are day trips with a break for a picnic lunch or with your own supply in the saddle bag.

Reservations should be made as far in advance as possible direct with the riding centre. You should state your age, riding ability, weight and your exact requirements. A deposit equivalent to 30 per cent is usually required. Before leaving the centre you should ensure that you know what you have paid for, such as board and lodging and baths, etc. If an animal is deemed to have been overworked or any tack is lost or damaged, the cost will be deducted from the deposit. Accommodation offered on equestrian holidays is often in modest *dortoirs* or dormitories along the *gîte d'étape* network of overnight hostels for riders, walkers and cyclists. But there are also trips which lay emphasis on enjoying the gastronomic delights of the region at the end of each day!

Another increasingly popular alternative is that of touring in horse-drawn caravans, Romany-style. Travel is at approximately 5 kmph, and this type of holiday has immediate and obvious appeal for horse-lovers, as well as allowing plenty of time to enjoy the delights of the countryside.

GOLF

THE GREEN HEART OF FRANCE

The recent upsurge of interest in the game throughout France is reflected in the creation of a number of courses in the Loire within the last few years. Often superbly designed, and always merging with the natural beauty of the countryside, they present a varying level of challenge to proficient golfers. The courses listed below are all 18-holers, and a range of hotels located close to the courses has also been included to enable visitors to incorporate their sporting pleasure with accommodation in hotels which, in some cases, offer discounts on green fees to their guests.

❶ Beaugency
Golf International les Bordes
Saint-Laurent-Nouan
41220 La Ferté-Saint-Cyr
☎ 54.87.72.13
South of Beaugency, follow D925 for 6 km
Par 72, 18-hole course designed by the American golf course architect, Robert von Hagge, and situated on a hunting estate bordering the Sologne. This course is not recommended for beginners since it incorporates many water hazards and is technically very challenging. Open all year, there is a pro shop, driving range and electric cart hire. Green fees 350FF on weekdays, 650FF at weekends. Bar and restaurant.
Accommodation
Self-catering maisonnettes (on site)
☎ 54.87.72.13

❷ Chartres
Golf du Château de Maintenon
route de Gallardon
28130 Maintenon
☎ 37.27.18.09
North of Chartres
In the grounds of the château, this 18-hole parkland course is a par 72 with natural features providing interesting golfing hazards. Green fees 210FF on weekdays for 18 holes, 140FF at weekends for 9 holes, with coaching available. Additionally there is a 9-hole practice course and driving range. Restaurant and bar and children's play area supervised at weekends.
Hotels
Hôtel du Château d'Esclimont ★★★
Saint Symphorien le Château
☎ 37.31.15.15
Hôtel Ibis ★★
place Drouaise
Chartres
☎ 37.36.06.36

❸ Cheverny
Golf du Château de Cheverny
La Rousselière
Cheverny
41700 Contres
☎ 54.79.24.70
in Cheverny
Built over a huge area bordering the Cheverny forest estate, this 18-hole course is par 71 and combines challenge with beauty. Green fees 180FF on weekdays, 250FF at weekends. There is a 3-hole practice course and driving range with a clubhouse bar and restaurant overlooking the lake. Coaching available.
Hotels
Hôtel du Domaine des Hauts de Loire ★★★★
route de Herbault
Onzain
☎ 54.20.72.57
Hôtel du Château du Breuil (on site) ★★★
route de Fougères
Cheverny
☎ 54.44.20.20
Hôtel l'Horset-la-Vallière ★★★
avenue Manoury, Blois
☎ 54.74.19.00
Hôtel Novotel ★★★
rue de l'Almandin
la Chaussée-Saint-Victor
☎ 54.78.33.57
Hôtel des Trois Marchands ★★
place de l'Eglise
Cour-Cheverny
☎ 54.79.96.44

❹ La Ferté-Saint-Aubin
Golf Club de la Plaine
Marcilly-en-Villette
45240 La Ferté-Saint-Aubin
☎ 38.76.11.73
Orléans to St-Cyr-en-Val then D108 towards Marcilly
In the Sologne forest region, this 18-hole par 72 course has been created with several water hazards and bunkers and has made use of a converted farmhouse for the clubhouse. Green fees 100FF on weekdays, 160FF at weekends, there is

GOLF

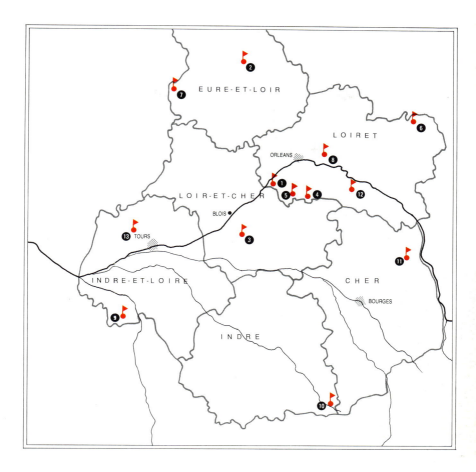

coaching, a 9-hole practice course and driving range. Pro shop, restaurant and bar. Open all year, closed Tues.
Hotels
Hôtel du Château des Muids ∗∗∗
Route Nationale 20
La Ferté-Saint-Aubin
☎ 38.64.65.14
Hôtel Novotel ∗∗∗
rue Honoré de Balzac
Orléans-la-Source
☎ 38.63.04.28
Hôtel Campanile ∗∗
rue de Chateaubriand
Orléans-la-Source
☎ 38.63.58.20
Hôtel du Perron ∗∗
9 rue du Maréchal Leclerc
La Ferté-Saint-Aubin
☎ 38.76.53.36
Auberge de la Croix Blanche ∗
place de l'Eglise
Marcilly-en-Villette
☎ 38.76.10.14

❺ La Ferté-Saint-Aubin
Golf Club de Sologne
Country Club des Olleries
route de Jouy-le-Potier
45240 La Ferté-Saint-Aubin
☎ 38.76.57.33

Orléans to La Ferté-Saint-Aubin then D18 towards Jouy-le-Potier
This 18-hole par 72 course runs through a forested estate with the typically watery landscape of the Sologne much in evidence. A 3-hole practice course, driving range, pro shop and tennis court add to the facilities with coaching available on request. Open all year; min handicap 35. Green fees 140FF on weekdays, 240FF at weekends. Bar and restaurant with children's nursery.
Accommodation
Chalet apartments and bedrooms in the château (on site)
☎ 38.76.57.33

❻ Montargis
Golf Club de Vaugouard
chemin des Bois
Fontenay-sur-Loing
45210 Ferrières-en-Gâtinais
☎ 38.95.81.52
North of Montargis in the direction of Fontenay-sur-Loing
Par 72, American-style 18-hole course with several interesting water hazards such as greens on islands and angled slopes and wooded fairways. Open all year; min handicap 35 on weekdays, 28 at weekends. Green fees 200FF on

THE DRYADES GOLF CLUB

weekdays, 330FF at weekends. The unique water-practice range is a feature and there is coaching available, Mar-Sep. Bar, restaurant, pro shop, five tennis courts, riding stables and a swimming pool and keep-fit centre add to the amenities.
Hotel
Hôtel du Domaine de
Vaugouard (on site) ***
chemin des Bois
☎ 38.95.71.85

❼ Nogent-le-Rotrou
Golf du Perche
Souancé-au-Perche
28400 Nogent-le-Rotrou
☎ 37.29.17.33
At Nogent-le-Rotrou, west of Chartres
Constructed amidst pleasant undulating countryside of ponds, orchards and valleys, the facilities include a par 72, 18-hole course and 3-hole practice course plus driving range. Pro shop with electric cart hire, bar, restaurant and children's nursery. Green fees 150FF on weekdays, 250FF at weekends, and coaching available. Closed Tues.
Hotel
Hôtel Interhotel Couronnet **
rue des Viennes
Nogent-le-Rotrou
☎ 37.52.85.00

❽ Orléans
Golf du Val de Loire
Château de la Touche
Donnery
45450 Fay-aux-Loges
☎ 38.59.25.15
15 km east of Orléans towards Montargis, in the direction of Donnery
Attractively laid-out par 72, 18-hole course set amidst woodland and presenting varying levels of challenge. Open all year, closed Tues, except Jul/Aug; min handicap 35. Green fees 180FF on weekdays, 250FF at weekends, coaching is available, Apr-Sep and there is also a driving range, pro shop, bar and restaurant.
Hotels
Hôtel Novotel ***
avenue de Verdun
Saint-Jean-de-Braye
☎ 38.84.65.65
Hôtel du Domaine de Chicamour **
Sury-aux-Bois
☎ 38.59.35.42

❾ Richelieu
Golf de Saint-Hilaire
Centre des Loisirs Loudun-Roiffé
86120 Les Trois Moutiers
☎ 49.98.78.06
On the D58 in the direction of Richelieu and Loudun
18-hole par 72 public course, in attractive woodland setting with 6-hole practice course, driving range and an impressive clubhouse building. Green fees 130FF on weekdays, 180FF at weekends. Min handicap 36, there is coaching available. Closed Tues, except Jul-Sep. Bar and restaurant, also tennis and fishing facilities.
Hotels
Hôtel du Château de Marcay ****
☎ 47.93.03.47
Hôtel Mercure **
☎ 49.98.19.22

❿ Sainte-Sévère-sur-Indre
Golf Club des Dryades
Pouligny-Notre-Dame
36160 Sainte-Sévère-sur-Indre
☎ 54.30.28.00
Châteauroux, then D943 in the direction of Pouligny-Notre-Dame
A well-constructed course of national and international standard, it is built on grounds overlooking the Vallée Noire, George Sand country. The 18-hole course is par 72 and includes several water

hazards. There is also a short 9-hole practice course and driving range, pro shop and electric cart hire. Open all year; min handicap 35. Green fees 100FF on weekdays, 150FF at weekends. Coaching is combined with fitness programmes run by the hotel which boasts a health and fitness institute. Clubhouse restaurant and tennis courts, additional restaurants in the associated hotel complex, with reductions in green fees for residents.

Hotel
Hôtel des Dryades (on site) ***
☎ 54.30.28.00

⑪ Sancerre
Golf du Sancerrois
Saint-Thibault-Saint-Satur
18300 Sancerre
☎ 48.54.11.22
Just north of Sancerre
On the banks of the Loire and with the Sancerrois hills in the background, this 18-hole par 71 course has water hazards, raised greens and a large number of bunkers. Min handicap 35 at weekends. Green fees 120-150FF on weekdays, 180-200FF at weekends; coaching available, Jun-Sep. There is also a driving range and 6-hole practice course, several tennis courts, two restaurants and a bar. Course closed Tues.

Hotel
Hôtel du Laurier **
29 rue du Commerce
Saint-Satur
☎ 48.54.17.20

THE ARDREE GOLF CLUB

⑫ Sully-Sur-Loire
Golf Club de Sully-sur-Loire
L'Ousseau-Viglain
45600 Sully-sur-Loire
☎ 38.36.52.08
8 km south-west of Sully, D120 towards Viglain
Close to the Sologne, this is an 18-hole par 72 course of international standard, plus three 9-hole practice courses and driving range. Open all year, closed Tues. Min handicap 28 for ladies, 24 for men, the course is open to beginners after 4 p.m. at weekends. Green fees 200FF on weekdays, 350FF at weekends. There is a pro shop, electric carts for hire and coaching available. Bar, restaurant and fully supervised children's nursery at weekends, open from Mar-Nov.

Hotels
Hostellerie du Grand Sully **
boulevard du Champ de Foire
Sully-sur-Loire
☎ 38.36.27.56
Hôtel du Pont de Sologne **
rue Porte du Sologne
Sully-sur-Loire
☎ 38.36.26.34
Hôtel de la Poste **
rue de Faubourg Saint-Germain
Sully-sur-Loire
☎ 38.36.26.22

⑬ Tours
Golf d'Ardrée
Saint-Antoine-du-Rocher
37360 Neuillé-Pont-Pierre
☎ 47.56.77.38
12 km north of Tours
In glorious parkland, this 18-hole, par 71 course is played between ancient trees and scattered water hazards. An additional 6-hole practice course and driving ranges complete the extensive facilities. Min handicap 36. Green fees 180-250FF on weekdays, 250-280FF at weekends, there is individual coaching on request. Open all year. Restaurant and bar.

Hotels
Hôtel du Domaine de Beauvois ****
Le Pont Clouet
Saint-Etienne-de-Chigny
☎ 47.55.50.11
Hôtel du Château de l'Aubrière ***
route de Fondettes
La Membrolle-sur-Choisille
☎ 47.51.50.35
Hôtel du Domaine des Hautes Roches ***
quai de la Loire
Rochecorbon
☎ 47.52.88.88
Hôtel Harmonie ***
15 rue Joliot-Curie
Tours
☎ 47.66.01.48
Hôtel Aster *
avenue du Mans
Saint-Cyr-sur-Loire
☎ 47.42.61.61

VINEYARDS

DISCOVERING AND VISITING A GREAT WINE REGION

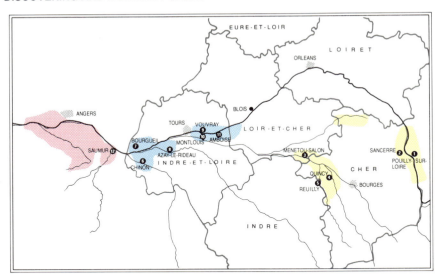

The Loire valley vineyards are particularly well placed along the banks of both the Loire and its tributaries, and the wines they produce are highly favoured by connoisseurs. Although the word 'Loire' does not always figure in their names, it is a useful geographical point of reference, indicating specific characteristics derived from the river and its soil. The vineyards fall into clearly defined sectors: Reuilly, Quincy, Menetou-Salon and Sancerre (in the *départements* of Indre and Cher) and Pouilly-sur-Loire, all in the river's upper reaches; the Touraine vineyards between Blois and Montsoreau; and then the Anjou and Saumur vineyards from Montsoreau to Ingrandes. Apart from these are the Coteaux du Loir and Coteaux de Jasnières vineyards to the north, and Muscadet to the west, in the lower reaches.

Like the Loire's famous châteaux, its wines and vineyards are acknowledged as elements in the historical and cultural heritage of the region, and an expression of its identity. Just as the air, the soil and the sun are fundamental to the vineyard, so it is the human skill and devotion which are essential to wine production. Excursions and visits along the vineyard routes offer delightful and picturesque landscapes as well as encounters with wine producers, whose hospitality is traditionally as renowned as their expertise.

Both the great estates or *domaines* and the small cooperative producers offer *dégustations* or tastings as well as the opportunity to purchase. The wine-making 'culture' has its museums too, with plenty of information on the alchemy of wine and the history of the wine-growing region; and there are festivals and fairs to give you a chance to join in local life and discover its traditions.

VINEYARDS OF THE UPPER LOIRE

The first vineyards entitled to use the 'Loire' name appear half-way along the river, between Nevers and Gien. Sancerre and Pouilly-sur-Loire lie along the hillsides by the Loire itself, with Menetou-Salon to the west on the River Saudre, Quincy on the Cher, and Reuilly on the Arnon.

❶ Pouilly-sur-Loire. Although these vineyards lie in the *département* of the Nièvre, their character links them to the Loire wines. The Sauvignon grape produces here an exceptional and justly famous wine, Pouilly-Fumé.

❷ Sancerre (whites, reds and rosés). The town of Sancerre perched on its knoll provides a magnificent panoramic view over the vine-clad hillsides and the little surrounding villages: St-Satur, Fontenay, Chavignol and Amigny. The local product is a famous dry white wine, the best known from the upper Loire.

❸ Menetou-Salon (whites, reds and rosés). West of Sancerre and 15 km north of Bourges, this small vineyard can trace its fame and reputation farther back in time than almost any other. In the 15th century it belonged to the famous Jacques Coeur, treasurer to Charles VII, a great traveller and skilled trader.

❹ Quincy (whites). The Quincy vineyards, 50 km from the river and 20 km from Bourges, cover the hill of the same

name, and also the hill of Brinay on the left bank of the Cher.
❺ *Reuilly* (whites, rosés and reds). Lying 10 km from Quincy on the banks of the River Arnon, this small and very ancient vineyard produces an interesting wine – though rare because of its limited production.

Suggested tours and visits
The Sancerre wine route makes a pleasant tour of villages and hamlets surrounded by vineyards. The Pouilly-sur-Loire wine route allows motorists to discover Les Loges, Château de Nozet, Bouchot, St Andelain, Tracy and the Château de Tracy, with the cellars at the Château de Nozet, the largest of these *domaines*, open to the public. The Sauvignon route can also take in the *domaine* of Pouilly-sur-Loire. It includes all the vineyards mentioned above as well as Valençay and Châteaumeillant, with its *vin gris*. All produce interesting VDQS wines and present an opportunity to discover the wine-producing country of the Berry region.
Details of *Routes des Vins* mentioned are available from the Comité départemental du Tourisme du Cher, 10 rue de la Chappe, Bourges ☎ 48.70.71.72.

VINEYARDS OF THE TOURAINE

Vines have been cultivated round Tours since ancient times. From the 4th century onwards, wine-making expanded under the guidance of St-Martin of Tours who is credited with the introduction of the most productive *cépage* or grape variety for white wine, the Pineau de Loire, otherwise known as *Chenin blanc*.
In the Middle Ages the spread of Christianity went hand in hand with the spread of the vine; kings and seigneurs endowed each new monastery with vineyards, and the monks' knowledge and perseverance in this difficult and demanding art soon made them the most skilful vine growers.
There is a legend that in AD 345 St-Martin, who is known to have travelled throughout the Church's wine-producing domains, left his donkey tethered close to a row of vines, where it nibbled the leaves and young shoots. The following year the cropped vinestock produced bunches of grapes of a better quality than its neighbours – thus the art of pruning is said to have been discovered by the monks, who lost no time in perfecting it.
Down the centuries the wines of Touraine were as greatly appreciated by the kings of France as by the great writers who were liberal with their praises. Rabelais, creator of Pantagruel, is responsible for the famous assessment of Vouvray wine: 'How good is God who gives us this fine wine, this good white Pineaulz . . . this is Pineau z wine, a good white wine! And by my faith, it is truly a taffeta wine.'
In the 19th century Touraine adopted the *champenoise* method of making sparkling wines and applied it to Vouvray, Montlouis and Touraine wines.
The vast territory of Touraine vineyards divides into seven main groups in two principal areas, totalling 10,350 hectares.

West of Tours
❻ *Chinon* (reds, whites, rosés). 1,500 hectares across the whole of the Véron area, watered by the River Vienne. The green hillsides laden with vines spread out on both sides of the river from l'île Bouchard to Chinon.
❼ *Bourgueil* and *St-Nicolas de Bourgueil* (reds and rosés). 1,900 hectares of vineyards on a 15-km terrace along the hillsides.
❽ *Touraine-Azay* (whites and rosés). 100 hectares beside the River Indre, dominated by the famous château of Azay-le-Rideau.

East of Tours
❾ *Vouvray* (whites). 1,800 hectares spread over eight communes round Vouvray. The vineyards climb the slopes on the right bank of the river, up to the escarpments with cellars hollowed out of the rock, used for storing the wine in barrels.
❿ *Montlouis* (whites). 300 hectares in three communes between the Loire and the Cher.
⓫ *Touraine-Amboise*, *Touraine-Mesland* (whites, rosés, and reds). Two small *domaines* of neighbouring *appellations*, totalling 450 hectares.
The area of wine production which bears the Touraine *appellation* (white, rosé and red wines) covers nearly 4,300 hectares spread throughout the region.

Suggested tours and visits
Lying at the heart of the Bourgueil and St-Nicolas vineyards is the 'Dive Bouteille' exhibition cellar, an impressive cellar carved out of the tufa rock and consisting of several halls and galleries. Here one can see two wine-presses of the 17th and 18th centuries and there is an important exhibition devoted to the vineyards and the art of vine-growing: conducted tours of all the local vineyards are also offered. Located at Chevrette (1 km from Bourgueil) it is open daily Feb-Apr and Oct-Nov 10–12 and 2–6. 1 May-30 Sep 10–12.30 and 2.30–7.30.
In 15th-century cellars the 'Musée Animé' of wine and cooperage at Chinon uses moving models to re-create the winemaker's ancient work-patterns accompanied by a recorded commentary. The visit ends with a wine-tasting. Located at 12 rue Voltaire, Chinon, it is open daily except Tues, 10–12 and 2–6 (until 7 from 1 Apr-31 Aug).

The Touraine Wine Museum and St-Julien wine cellars cover the history of wine and wine-growers, the alchemy of wine-making and man's love for wine in life, literature and song. Located at 12–16 rue Nationale, Tours, it is open daily except Tuesdays, 9–12 and 2–5.
1 Apr-30 Sept, 9–12 and 2.7. Closed on national holidays ☎ 47.61.07.93.
Seven different tours (60 km and 150 km) combine historic sites, attractive scenery and panoramic views and the important wine-growing centres of the Touraine. Further information from CIVT, Maison des Vins de Touraine, 19 square Prosper-Mérimée, Tours ☎ 47.05.40.01. The Bourgueil wines route (60 km) runs through magnificent scenery, from the banks of the Loire to the vineyards. Details from the Tourist Office, Mairie de Bourgueil ☎ 47.97.70.50.

Wine fairs and festivals
Amboise: Easter.
Azay-le-Rideau: last Sat in Feb.
Bourgueil and St-Nicolas: 2–3 Mar.
Chinon: second weekend in Mar.
Montlouis: 27–28 Apr.
Thésée: 27–28 Apr and 15 Aug.
Vouvray: 2–3 Feb and 15 Aug.

VINEYARDS OF ANJOU AND SAUMUR

There are references to the vineyards of Anjou and Saumur as early as the 5th and 6th centuries, when Sidoine Apollinaire sang the praises of Angers 'rich in the offerings of Ceres and Bacchus', and Gregory of Tours, an historian and lover of good wines, referred in his writings to their extensive terrain. The Carolingian kings Pépin le Bref (715–768), Charlemagne (742–814), and Charles the Bald (823–877) were the first famous proprietors.
The vineyards were of economic importance by the 12th and 13th centuries; their wines were exported to England by the Plantagenets – Counts of Anjou – and then by King Philippe Auguste (1165–1223), although he kept the best wines for the French Court.
Trade with the Netherlands developed in the 13th century and some of the finest wines, those which could best withstand the rigours of the journey, were shipped there. They were defined for this reason as 'sea wines', the 'land wines' being those sent to Paris.
The latter were just as good as the wines selected for export, and their nickname of the 'little Anjou wines' marked the beginning of their widespread fame.
The 16th century saw this fame grow thanks to the exceptional quality of the great white wines which inspired the poet Joachim Du Bellay (1522–1560) to write:

May the fragrant juices
Of the spreading vine
Ripen in the sunlight
Of thine eye divine,
And sweeten like the nectar
Of my sweet Anjou wine.

In the 17th century, the Abbé-Breton introduced the Cabernet Franc grape into the Loire region from Bordeaux in order to improve the red wine varieties. One of these is the now renowned 'Saumur Champigny'.
The Layon canal was built by Louis XVI (1754–1793) so that the ships of the Compagnie des Indes – the French equivalent of England's East India Company – could penetrate inland to load up with barrels.
Here too, introduction of the *champenoise* method in the 19th century led to production of two sparkling wines, the 'Brut de Saumur' and 'Crémant de Loire'. The vineyards cover 20,000 hectares from Saumur to Ingrandes, beyond Angers, mostly on the slopes of the left bank of the Loire and those of its tributaries whose names they often bear.

⓬ *Saumur* and *Saumur-Champigny* (whites, red) wines come from both banks of the Thouet. The *Saumur-Champigny* vineyards produce the best red wines of Anjou and Saumur and are situated in the triangle between the Loire and its placid tributary the Thouet.
The left bank has the largest local cellars used for the champagne method of production of the white sparkling Saumur, and almost everywhere cellars are cut into the rock for wine storage.
Production of rosé wines is spread across the whole region, with four main divisions: rosés d'Anjou, rosés de Loire (appellations), cabernet d'Anjou and cabernet de Saumur.
The *Coteaux de l'Aubance* vineyards (whites), cover the riverside slopes of the River Aubance as it flows peacefully through gentle valleys.
The *Coteaux du Layon* vineyards (whites) are scattered over some 50 km from Doué-la-Fontaine to Chalonnes. Visitors can follow the winding river down through the hills, passing one wine-producing village after another until it reaches the Loire.
The *Anjou Coteaux de la Loire* vineyards (whites) spread out to the south-west of Angers, on both sides of the river, with those of the *Savennières* (whites) on the right bank. The latter are well worth a detour, as much for the impressive landscape of rocky spurs crowned with vines which advance towards the river, as for the pretty village of Savennières itself.

Suggested tours and visits
Angers and Saumur are the region's chief

wine-making centres. Each has its *Maison du Vin*, a centre for information, documentation on wines and vineyards, and a selection of the finest wines available for tasting. Maison du Vin de Saumur, 25 rue Beaurepaire, Saumur ☎ 41.51.16.60. Maison du Vin de l'Anjou, 5 bis place Kennedy, Angers ☎ 41.88.81.13.

The Anjou wine route is full of charm and attraction, winding through the vineyards and pretty villages of Anjou and the Saumur region, from historic châteaux to wine-cellars. A random selection of places might include the château de Barbe-Bleue or Blue-beard's Castle at Champtocé, reminders of the poet Joachim du Bellay at Liré, wine-press manufacturing at Chalonnes, the wine-growers' village of La Haie-Longue with its old houses, the beautiful village of Beaulieu-sur-Layon and its combined museum and tasting cellar, Brissac's 12th-century tasting cellar at the château, and the many cellars tunnelled in the local tufa rock, which you reach by driving into the enormous galleries. Details from the Maison du Vin, Angers.

For those interested in sparkling wines, the double village of St-Hilaire-St-Florent, spread out between the Loire and the slopes 3 km north-west of Saumur, specializes in the champagne method, and there are cellars open to visitors in the former tufa quarries.

Wine fairs and festivals
Distre: *vendange* (wine harvest) festival, second Sun in Oct.
Meigne-le-Vicomte: wine and cheese fair, second Sun in May.
Le Puy-Notre-Dame: wine and mushroom festival, first weekend in July.
St-Aubin-de-Luigne: wine and eel festival, third weekend in July.
Saumur: fair, second weekend in Feb.
Thouarcé: wine festival of Thouarcé and Bonnezeaux, first weekend in Sep.

WORK IN THE VINEYARDS AND CELLARS

Planting and propagation
Young shoots cut off while the vine is dormant during the autumn and winter (the vine-shoot harvest) are kept in sand until the spring. When the young plants have put down roots, after a year, they are planted out to replace worn-out vine-stocks, or in new sites.
The *cépage* indicates the grape varieties. In the Loire valley the chief varieties are Cabernet franc (red and rosé), Cabernet Sauvignon and Groslot (rosé d'Anjou), Chenin blanc (both Anjou and Touraine white), Sauvignon blanc (white in the upper Loire, Pouilly-Fumé, Sancerre).

Harvest
October is the month for the Loire valley *vendange* or harvest.
Red wines are made from black grapes. As soon as the fruit is picked, the grapes are stripped off the bunches and tipped into fermentation vats. The maceration time varies for each type of wine: four or five days for a *primeur* wine to be drunk while still young, two to three weeks for a wine which is to be laid down. By the end of the fermentation, pulp and skins have sunk to the bottom of the vats and form the '*marc*', which is pressed to yield a wine '*de presse*'. The '*vin libre*' – the unpressed wine – continues to mature in vats for between one and two months for '*primeurs*', and for up to one or two years for long-keeping wines. It is racked several times, a process whereby the wine is drawn off into another vat, leaving behind the successive lees which it deposits. Clarification is accelerated by fining and filtering for wines which will be moved into bottles very early, but occurs naturally with wines which remain in the vat for long periods. For rosé wines the black grapes undergo a very short maceration (only 24 hours) before being pressed and moved into the vat. The wine is bottled the following spring. For a *vin gris*, a 'grey wine', the black grapes are pressed immediately, without maceration.
White Loire wines are made from white grapes and black grapes with white juice (in Anjou), or from white grapes alone (in Touraine and the vineyards upstream). The grapes are pressed gently, without previous maceration, to obtain high-quality juice. This is then fermented in barrels in cool cellars, at 14°–15° Celsius. Dry white wines are bottled young, after twelve to eighteen months in the barrel, and need only a few rackings. Sweet white wines require grapes which are very rich in sugar, not all of which will convert to alcohol: this characteristic is encouraged by late harvesting, allowing the grapes to mature until they are subject to '*pourriture noble*' or noble rot; this is the result of a fungus or mould, *Botrytis cinerea*, which produces a loss of liquid in the fruit and thus a greater concentration of sugars.
The '*champenoise*' or champagne method is applied to wines with a naturally sparkling tendency. The wine, with added sugar or '*tirage*' liquor, achieves a second fermentation over two months, in bottles, resulting in a '*prise de mousse*', the developing sparkle. The wine continues to mature in the bottle for another nine months, still on its yeasty lees. During the next phase, the '*remuage*', each bottle is turned every day for two months; at the end of this time the deposit has settled against the cork. The final '*dégorgement*' consists of removing this deposit and replacing the cork, while losing as little sparkle as possible.

MOTORING TOURS

This chapter suggests some itineraries to help you explore the Loire valley region by region. We have chosen minor roads, where possible, to make the journey more pleasant for drivers and less arduous for cyclists – for whom we also offer a couple of shorter outings. These routes connect up the main historic sites and places of interest. They also take you to many lesser-known châteaux and charming small villages typical of this part of France. For each itinerary we have indicated a number of 'staging posts': towns where you will find good restaurants and hotel accommodation. Most of these and the main features for which the town is noted are listed in the 'Gazetteer' section.

Ranging from 90 km to 180 km in length, these drives can be varied to suit individual taste. You can go at your own speed, making a rapid tour with just a glance at some of the places of interest, or spending several leisurely days, stopping as you please, and deviating from the suggested route if you feel like it.

All the maps in this section are 1:250,000. To help you pinpoint the starting point of each drive, map references are provided relating to the atlas.

CASTLES AND CAVES AMONG THE VINEYARDS

90 km
Map ref.
127 D5

This circuit takes you through wine-growing country in search of castles, an abbey, and some strange cave dwellings. Suggested staging-posts are Saumur, Fontevraud, Montreuil-Bellay and Gennes-les-Rosiers.

Begin with a look at **Saumur**. Standing out above the rooflines, the château marks the old town area, with narrow streets leading from the banks of the Loire, where you pass Renaissance houses and 18th-century mansions. Besides the collections in the château's two museums, those of fine arts and harness-making, there are 16th-century tapestries in the Romanesque and Flamboyant style church of Notre-Dame-de-Nantilly, the *Maison du Vin de Saumur* in rue Beaurepaire, and the cavalry museum in avenue Foch to visit. On the other side of the Cessart bridge is the Ile Offard, on which stands an elegant 15th-century mansion, known as the 'House of the Queen of Sicily'.

Before setting off towards **Montsoreau**, make a 1-km detour south to the Bagneux dolmen, Europe's biggest megalith. The minor roads between Saumur and Montsoreau pass through charming villages, vineyards, wine cellars and, at Souzay-Champigny, Turquant and Parnay, neolithic cave dwellings. (You can walk the 3.5 km from Dampierre to Parnay on a waymarked path, the Grande Randonnée GR3 route, running through vineyards). One km south-west of Montsoreau stands the 15th-century windmill of La Herpinière, in a remarkable state of preservation. Break your journey at Montsoreau and enjoy a delightful

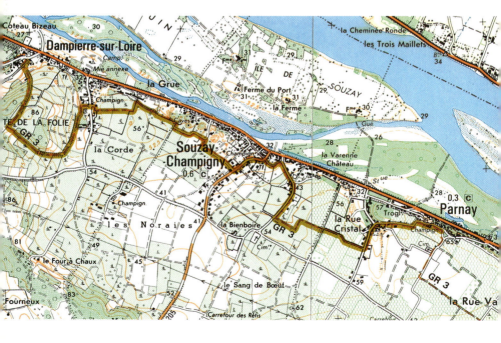

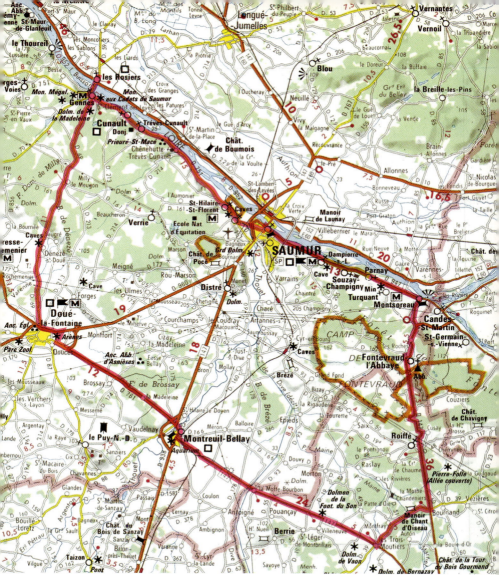

panorama of hillsides clad with vines and fruit trees. A visit to the château here may remind you of the story of the Lady of Montsoreau, recounted with poetic licence by Alexandre Dumas.
Some 4.5 km south on the D947 is **Fontevraud-l'Abbaye**, in whose superb abbey church, known as the 'Grand Moustier', are the tombs of Henry II of England, Eleanor of Aquitaine and their son, Richard the Lionheart.
Continue southwards, passing Pierre-Folle, whose tree-lined avenue, accessible only on foot, is a charming place for a stroll. A few kilometres further on, you pass the elegant manor of Chant d'Oiseau before entering a region famed for its dolmens, at Barnazay, Vernaise, Vaon and Fontaine du Son. Then you turn north-westwards to the small fortified town of **Montreuil-Bellay**, with its four monumental gateways and mighty fortress on the banks of the Thouet, an ideal spot for walks or fishing.
Next take the D761 to **Doué-la-Fontaine**, a centre for rose growing amidst another area of prehistoric cave dwellings – at Rochemenier, La Fosse and Denezé-sous-Doué – with a zoo park, sited in former quarries, where the animals are free to roam in large enclosures. From there the D69 runs through more wine-growing villages to **Gennes-les-Rosiers**, where there are both neolithic and classical remains: the Dolmen de la Madeleine, and a Roman amphitheatre and aqueduct.
Returning towards Saumur on the D751, you come to **Cunault**, whose admirable medieval church is austerely Romanesque. Then you can stop in the twin villages of **St-Hilaire-St-Froment** to visit cellars where the local sparkling wine is produced, and make a short detour to the Ecole Nationale d'Equitation, the national riding school, on the Terrefort plateau, only 2 km from Saumur, where a one-hour guided tour gives you an insight into the art of horse-riding as practised by the renowned 'Cadre Noir'.

LAND OF RONSARD, RABELAIS AND BALZAC

110 km
Map ref.
129 C5

This tour explores the country between Tours and Chinon, an area rich in associations with French writers, and one which also boasts magnificent châteaux and excellent wines. Suggested staging posts are Tours, Savonnières, Langeais, Azay-le-Rideau, Bourgueil, Chinon and Montbazon.

Tours, chief city of the region, has many historical buildings. North-east of the town are the Château Royal, the Musée des Beaux-Arts (which houses the Grévin historical waxwork museum), and the cathedral of St-Gatien, which has an admirable 15th-century façade and some fine 13th-century stained glass. At 25 rue Colbert stands the Hôtel Goüin, whose light and airy façade is adorned with delicately chiselled ornamentation, and in the same district is the Musée du Compagnonnage, featuring the old guild system, and the Musée des Vins.

Three km to the west, between the Loire and the Cher, stands the priory of St-Cosme, last resting place of the poet Ronsard. Not far away is the Château de Plessis-les-Tours, favourite residence of Louis XI.

Ten km farther on, you cross the Cher to the village of **Savonnières**, where there are fantastic limestone caves with stalactites, a lake and waterfalls, and 'petrified' reconstructions of prehistoric fauna. The D7 leads on to the Château de Villandry, whose ornamental gardens on three levels are of international renown, and continues to Lignières, where you take the D57 across to the north bank of the Loire and **Langeais**, dominated by its 15th-century castle which houses a collection of Flanders and Aubusson tapestries.

Now re-cross the Loire and continue along the D57, through vineyards, then along the bank of the Indre, to the captivating and typically Renaissance château of **Azay-le-Rideau**, built on piles driven into the river bed.

Cross the Indre and take the road running between the river and the forest of Chinon (D17 and D7), until you reach the Château d'Ussé, a rambling, fairy-tale castle combining 15th, 16th and 17th-century styles. At the junction of Indre and Loire stands the Chinon nuclear power station, where you cross the Loire again and drive northwards towards Bourgueil. A short detour to the left brings you to the Château de Réaux, a delightful architectural caprice and, farther on, to the village of **Chouzé-sur-Loire**, formerly a fishing port and now a windsurfing centre. At **Bourgueil** itself, the abbey is worth a visit, and a kilometre away, at Chevrette, the 'Cave Touristique de la Dive Bouteille' reminds us that we are in Rabelais country, where one of the best red wines

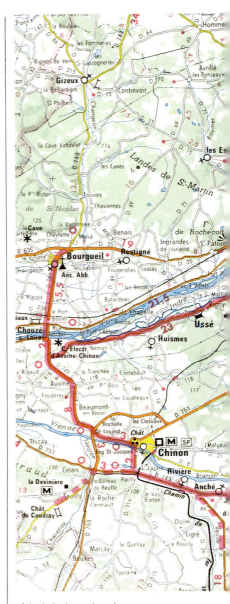

of the Loire is produced.

Re-cross the Loire and follow the D749 into **Chinon**, a town where ancient streets such as rue Haute-Saint-Maurice and Jeanne-d'Arc are lined with fine examples of 16th and 17th-century domestic architecture. The Hôtel des Etats Généraux houses the Musée de Vieux Chinon et de la Batellerie, a museum devoted to Chinon's history and its water transport. Dominating the little town are the ramparts, enclosing three fortresses separated by deep ditches: the ruins of Fort St-Georges, the Château du Milieu (a royal residence) and the Château de Coudray which houses a collection of gemstones. From Chinon, you can visit the Rabelais museum at La Devinière, and catch a glimpse of the châteaux of

MOTORING TOURS 41

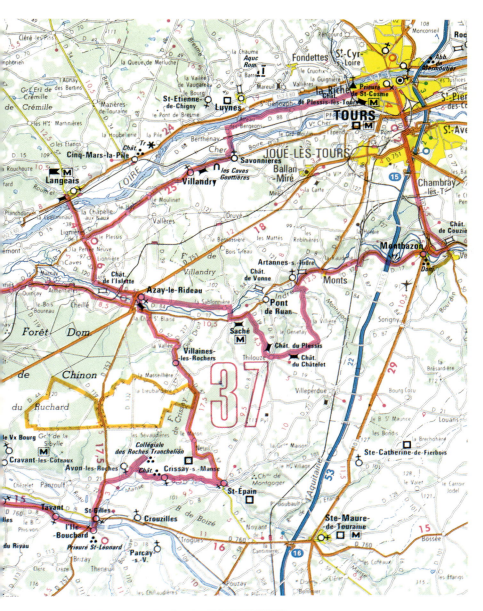

WINE MUSEUM, BOURGUEIL

Coudray-Montpensier and La-Roche-Clermault. Chinon is also the starting point for an interesting excursion: a ride on a steam railway south to Richelieu via Ligré and Champigny.
The route then follows the Vienne south-eastwards by the D749, then the D760 to **L'île-Bouchard**, where it is joined by the Manse. The town owes its name to the island at its centre, on which a fortress once stood. All that remains of the priory of St-Léonard is the apse and its chapels, with some fine sculpted capitals.
Here we leave the Vienne to explore the valley of the Manse via the D21. The first place of interest is 'Les Roches de Tranchelion', where the High-Gothic ruins of a collegiate church nudge the remains of an old fortress. At St-Epain, turn on to

the D57 and proceed to **Villaines-les-Rochers**, a village specializing in basket-making. Joining the D17, you reach the banks of the Indre again, not far from **Saché** whose château now houses the Balzac museum. You can make a detour via the D19 to reach the charming village of **Artannes-sur-Indre**, passing the châteaux of Valesne, Le Plessis and Le Châtelet, or follow the D17 along the river via Pont-de-Ruan. From Artannes, follow the wooded banks of the Indre to **Montbazon**, which has a striking 12th-century keep. There are charming minor roads in the vicinity of the château of Cozières and La Belle Jonchère, where water-mills and old wash houses will tempt you to linger by the river before going back to Tours. (You can in fact walk the 3 km between Montbazon and Veigné on the bank of the Indre, following the waymarked GR46 route.)

HISTORIC CHATEAUX IN TOURAINE

120 km
Map ref.
130 C2

This tour takes in Amboise, Chenonceaux, Loches and a number of the historical châteaux in the vicinity of Tours. Suggested staging posts are Amboise, Loches and Montlouis-sur-Loire.
Amboise has been the scene of major events in French history, and its splendid château was the residence of Charles VIII, Louis XII and François I, each of whom built additions according to his taste. Nearby is the Clos Lucé, the fine residence given by François I to Leonardo da Vinci, now housing a museum of his drawings and models of the futuristic machines he conceived. There is also a postal museum housed in the Hôtel de Joyeuse, a Renaissance building with a charming garden in matching style and, just outside the town, the tall Pagoda of Chanteloup, with a fine all-round view from the top.
From here the D31 runs through the forest of Amboise and past vine-clad hillsides to **Bléré**, where you join the D40 and drive along the Cher to **Chenonceau**, where the charming château is half palace, half bridge.
Before the next stop, **Montrichard**, you can drive north to enjoy the coolness of the Grand Etang de Jumeaux in the heart of the forest, or go boating on the Etang de la Brosse, 6 km to the south.
In the area between the Cher and Indre are three châteaux of like-sounding names but dissimilar appearance. Montrichard on the banks of the Cher, reached via the D40, is a 12th-century fortress with fine views from its high keep and the old town sprawling at its feet – a pleasant place to stroll. Fifteen km to the south on the D764, in woodland, stands Montpoupon, with a 15th-century main building and 16th-century postern gate. Drive on into the valley of the Indrois, shaded by the immense forest of Loches. The D10 follows the sleepy river through the villages of Genillé and Chemillé-sur-Indrois, until the Château de Montrésor appears on the horizon, like a sentry posted on a headland. From Montrésor, take the D760 through the forest, passing the manor of La Corroirie and the Carthusian monastery of Liget before emerging into the valley of the Indre, just outside **Loches**.
Start your tour of the town with a look at the old buildings in Beaulieu-lès-Loches, 1 km to the east. Entering Loches itself by the Porte des Cordeliers, you are immediately in the old town near the Tour St-Antoine. Walking up the hill, you come to the Porte Royale giving access to the extensive medieval walls which embrace the château, the church of St-Ours and the keep of the old fortress.
Continuing along the Indre on minor roads and the D17, you pass through the charming village of **Azay-sur-Indre**, whose diminutive château faces the manor of La

Follaine across the river. The next stop is **Cormery**, where remnants of its ruined abbey crop up all over the village. (You can walk the 5 km between Cormery and **Courçay**, following the waymarked GR46 route, with the river on one side and the forest on the other. Just beyond Courçay is the curious natural feature of 'Les Rochers'.) Driving north on the D82, you come to the Cher again, in wine-growing country, and the châteaux of Nitray, Leugny, La Bourdaisière and La Gravelle. Going on to **Montlouis**, you can visit neolithic cave dwellings now used for storing wine, before taking the D751 back along the Loire to Amboise.

AMBOISE CHATEAU

VENDÔME AND THE LOIR VALLEY

90 km
Map ref.
120 D3

This gentle excursion along the Loir (not the Loire!) will appeal especially to nature lovers; the banks of this quiet, meandering river are ideal for walks. The easy terrain of this itinerary is also suitable for cyclists. Suggested staging posts are Vendôme, Trôo and Montoire-sur-le-Loir.

Vendôme is a pleasant place for a stroll. The old town lies between two branches of the river, with a number of lesser channels, so the narrow streets are connected by a series of bridges. Wander from the Porte d'eau to the abbey, from the Tour St-Martin to the garden of the Hôtel du Saillant (now the Tourist Office), and from the church of La-Madeleine to the Porte St-Georges, before venturing over to the château on the farther bank. The most important building is the Abbaye de la Trinité, its spires and towers dominating this part of the town. The abbey church itself, a mixture of architectural styles, contrasts with the purely Romanesque bell tower. The former convent now houses a museum of religious art.

From Vendôme, follow the minor roads along the left bank of the Loir to **Lavardin**, 15 km distant. The village is dwarfed by the ruins of an old castle, currently being restored, on a rocky spur with fine views over the valley. As you approach **Couture-sur-Loir**, stop to admire the manor of La Possonnière, birthplace of the poet Ronsard, or enjoy the cool freshness of the Isle Verte. After a stop at **La Chartre-sur-le-Loir**, with its wine cellars and former leper hospice, cross to the other bank and return upstream by the D305 to **Poncé-sur-le-Loir**, whose outwardly modest château conceals within it an elaborate staircase.

Ten km further east via the D917, the village of **Trôo** is set on a hillside pockmarked with the tunnels of former quarry workings. From the collegiate church of St-Martin above the village there are magnificent views in every direction. **Montoire-sur-le-Loir**, 6.5 km farther on, is well worth visiting for the chapel of St-Gilles with its striking murals, Renaissance town houses in the place Georges Clémenceau and perhaps a walk along the river bank in a setting of greenery and flowers. The lakes south-east of the town form another cool, relaxing spot. Four km to the north, the hillsides overlooking **Les Roches-l'Evêque** are riddled with caves and neolithic cave dwellings. The charming village of Lunay on the D53, Gué-du-Loir with its Château de Bonaventure, and Villiers-sur-le-Loir (D5) are the final stages on the way back to Vendôme.

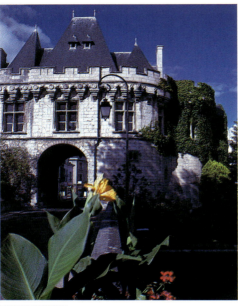

VENDOME CHATEAU

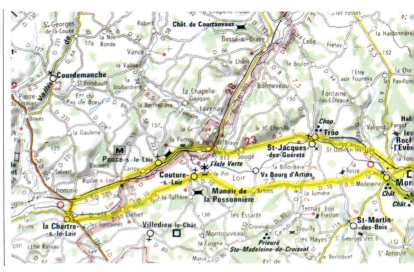

PALACES, PARKS AND FORESTS OF BLOIS

100 km
Map ref. 121 F5

This circuit runs through the rich, well-wooded country around Blois, taking in châteaux big and small, parks and forests. Suggested staging posts are Blois itself, Bracieux and Candé-sur-Beuvron.

Blois was one of the main centres of the Renaissance in France, its brilliance outlasting that of nearby Amboise. The town became a crown possession and its château was a favourite residence of many kings and queens. Sensitive restoration work was carried out in the 19th century, and the various ranges of buildings form an astonishing ensemble of different styles now housing the Musée

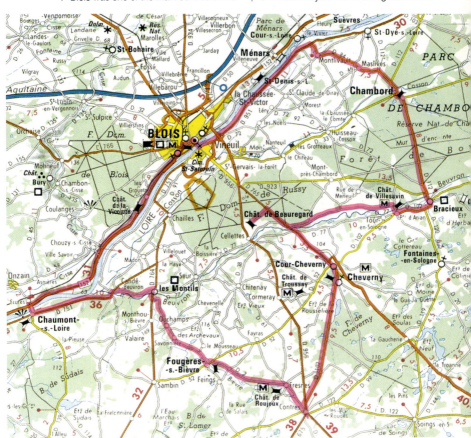

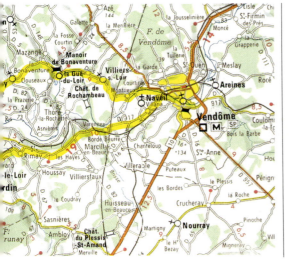

des Beaux-Arts, which includes portraits and mural paintings from the 16th and 17th centuries, and the private chamber of Catherine de' Medici, decorated with 237 carved wooden panels.
To the east of the château lies the old town. Note particularly the church of St-Nicolas, the Hôtel Alluye in the rue St-Honoré, the Hôtel Saunery and the Maison des Acrobates in the place St-Louis, and the rues St-Lubin, Robert Houdin, Pierre-de-Blois, des Papegaults, du Puits-Chatel and du Grenier-à-Sel. Behind the town hall are the gardens of the bishop's palace, with a fine panoramic view. Outside the town, near Vineuil, the Lac de Loire leisure centre has facilities for watersports, a swimming pool and a campsite.
To reach **Chambord**, follow the D951 for about 10 km, then turn right on to the D84. The colossal château stands in

CHAUMONT CHATEAU

splendid isolation with no town to its name, but surrounded by a wooded park of 5,550 hectares or 13,600 acres, most of it a hunting reserve. On the bank of the River Cosson, this château marks the high point of the Italianate Renaissance in the Loire valley, conceived by the 'builder king', as François I was known, as a grandiose hunting lodge. A simpler but no less impressive sight can be enjoyed in the park at dusk, when deer and wild boar come to drink at watering points, where hides enable visitors to observe them in their natural setting.

From Chambord take the D112 through the park and the forest of Boulogne, until you come to the picturesque old village of **Bracieux**, a good place to stroll and rest. Not far away on the D102 is the Château de Villesavin, country seat of Jean Le Breton, finance minister to François I, who diverted workmen and materials from the construction at Chambord to his own private building project. His mansion features high dormer windows with carved human figures, a spiral staircase, marble pool, and ornamental inscriptions on the façade. Now follow the minor roads along the Beuvron to the Château de Beauregard, on the fringe of the forest of Russy, which houses a portrait gallery of 363 kings and queens, courtiers and courtesans, from the 14th to the 17th centuries – history in pictures. Rejoin the D765 south-eastwards to **Cheverny**, a 17th-century château in the classical style. The most famous pack of hounds in France is kept in the kennels of Cheverny: seventy dogs of mixed Anglo-French pedigree.

From Cheverny, follow the D102 to **Contres**, a charming village set amidst vineyards, then take the D7 along the Bièvre as far as **Fougères-sur-Bièvre**. By virtue of its 11th-century keep, gate towers and machicolations, the château here might be termed a fortress, but it was embellished in the 15th century by the addition of Renaissance dormers and pinnacles and a hexagonal external staircase, and remodelled again in the 18th century with enlarged windows and sculpted doorways. Continue on the same road to **Candé-sur-Beuvron**, a good place to try the local cuisine, before taking the D751 to **Chaumont-sur-Loire**.

The village of Chaumont is overshadowed by its exquisite château on the slope above the river, its decorations including a frieze carved with the monograms of Charles and Catherine of Amboise. The site of the former north wing commands wide views over the Loire and its valley. From **Onzain**, on the further bank, you can make a one-hour boat trip downstream to **Amboise** before returning to Blois by the D751.

CHAMBORD CHATEAU

MOTORING TOURS 47

THE SOLOGNE, CHER AND FRINGES OF BERRY

100 km
Map ref.
131 C6

This circuit takes in three different types of country: the Sologne, the valley of the Cher and the northern fringes of the Berry region. Suggested staging posts are Romorantin-Lanthenay and Valençay. The little town of **Romorantin-Lanthenay** can be considered the capital of the **Sologne**, a strange region of sandy soils and heathland, meres, rivers and forests. The old town sits astride the River Sauldre, inviting you to linger on its bridges and explore its narrow streets. Old buildings include the small 15th to 16th-century Château Royal, the Chancellerie and 16th-century Maison du Carroir Doré. If you want to learn more about this unusual region, visit the Musée de la Sologne. On leaving the town, drive along the bank of the Sauldre (D724) to Pruniers-en-Sologne, and take the D128 across the valley of the Cher to **Chabris**, where you can hire canoes. Then follow the D4 to **Valençay**, on the edge of the Berry region.
Set on a hill with extensive views over the surrounding country, Valençay's château was built in the 16th century by the

VALENCAY CHATEAU

d'Etampes family. Later it belonged to Napoleon Bonaparte's minister, Talleyrand, which explains the predominance of the Empire style in the furnishings and interior decoration. (You can walk from Valençay to Veuil, 4 km to the south, along a marked bridle-way which follows the course of the Nahon. The scenery is delightful. Half way along is the Tour de Breuil. Veuil itself has a Romanesque church with 16th-century additions and a Renaissance château

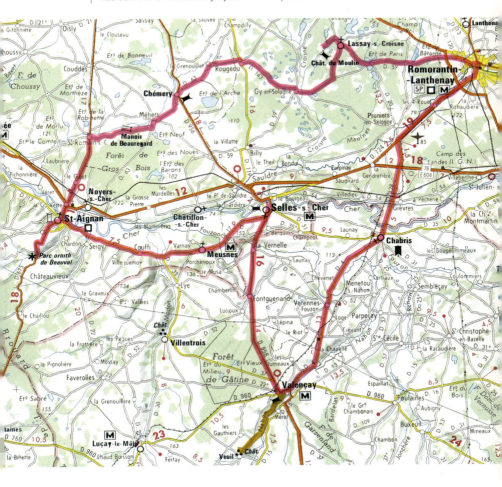

dominating the village.) Take the D956 through the forest of Gâtine with its two lakes. The road rejoins the Cher at **Selles**, a picturesque little town, in a wide bend of the river which feeds the moat of its château. Next, take the D17 south to Meusne, which has a charming Romanesque church, and on to **St-Aignan**, built on a hillside in the shadow of a 16th-century Renaissance château. At the foot of the hill stands the fine Romanesque collegiate church, its crypt beautifully decorated with frescoes. Two km to the south, the bird sanctuary at **Beauval** is home to a vast number of exotic species. At Ile-Plage near St-Aignan, you can hire canoes and paddle down the Cher as far as Montrichard.

From St-Aignan, take the D675 to St-Romain-sur-Cher, then turn off eastwards. The road follows the edge of the Gros Bois forest, passes the manor of Beauregard, then enters a wine-growing area near **Chemery**, a village which boasts its own small château. Now back in the Sologne, the road passes through woodland and beside lakes, big and small. Lassay-sur-Croisne, for instance, lies midway between the Château de Moulin, 2 km to the east, and the vast Etang Bézard to the north-west, and this sort of landscape continues on the 10 km back to Romorantin-Lanthenay.

MOTORING TOURS

THE LOIRE FROM ORLEANS TO GIEN

180 km
Map ref.
123 C4

This itinerary takes in the whole of the 'Orléanais' region. To the south loom the vast forests of the Sologne; to the north the forêt d'Orléans. Suggested staging posts are Orléans, Olivet, Sully-sur-Loire, Briare, Gien, Châteauneuf-sur-Loire and Combreux.

Of the major towns on the Loire **Orléans** is nearest to Paris, just 100 km south of the capital. The old quarters along the river and around the Sainte-Croix cathedral contain remarkable buildings from almost every period. In the south-east of the old town, near the waterfront, is the cloister of St-Aignan, rebuilt by Louis XI in the 15th

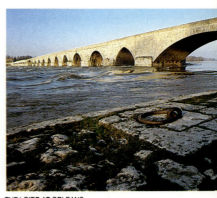
THE LOIRE AT ORLEANS

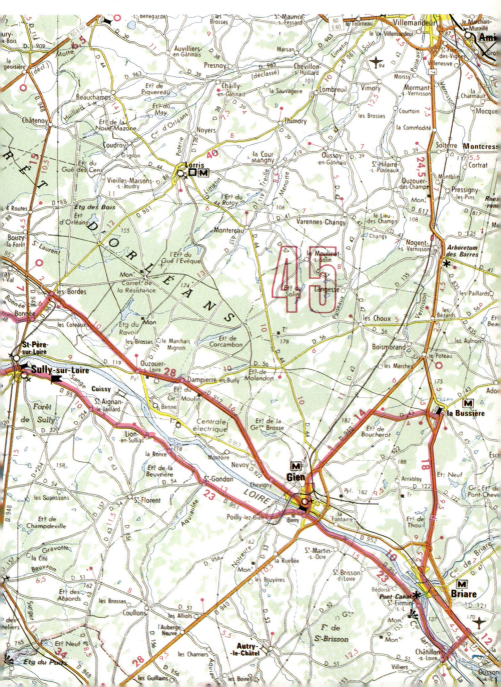

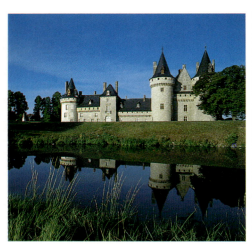

SULLY-SUR-LOIRE CHATEAU

century over a crypt dating from the 10th and 11th centuries with sculpted capitals to its pillars. In the same square is a 15th-century brick-built house where Louis XI is said to have stayed. Three streets farther on, the towers and delicate Gothic spire of the cathedral soar above the old town. The present building is not original, having been reconstructed during the 17th to 19th centuries. Its crypt contains Gallo-Roman, Carolingian and Roman remains from earlier buildings on the site. In the place de l'Etape stands the 16th-century Renaissance Hôtel Groslot, now the town hall, its white and honey-coloured stone façade set off by a roof of dark slate. Inside, rooms furnished in period style are open to visitors.

In the centre of town you should see the Pavillon de la Vieille Intendance, a Renaissance town house in the rue de la Bretonnerie, the Maison des Oves and its curious façade in the rue Sainte-Anne, the 17th-century town houses and 16th-century church in the rue d'Escures, and in the place du Martroi, two classical buildings which frame the entrance to the rue Royale. Between the place De Gaulle and the rue Tabor are the 15th-century Maison Jeanne d'Arc, with exhibits relating to her exploits; the Centre Charles Peguy, a museum and library devoted to this locally born poet; and in the rue Notre-Dame-de-Recouvrance the 16th-century Hôtel Toutin. Also worth seeing are the Hôtel des Créneaux, the Hôtel Cabu Museum of Orléanais archaeology and history, the Maison du Cerceau, Maison Alibert and Maison de la Coquille. Finally, the île Charlemagne is a pleasant spot to relax and, if you wish, enjoy watersports.

Four km south of Orléans by minor roads, you cross the Loiret and come to the quiet town of **Olivet**. The river bank, lined with water mills and pleasant houses, is an inviting spot for a stroll. (If you do decide on a walk, start from the Tourist Office, go north along the avenue de Loiret, cross the river, then turn left on to the river bank by the floral clock. Down beside the river are open-air cafés and water mills shaded by clumps of trees.) From Olivet, take the D14 to the flower gardens of **Orléans-la-Source**, where the Loiret rises, a fragrant oasis of greenery and colourful blossom. Continue along the D14, where a number of small châteaux shelter in the woodland fringes of the Sologne. The D14 eventually becomes the D951, which rejoins the main river at **Sully-sur-Loire**, whose 14th-century château was enlarged in the 16th century. From its park, on the tongue of land between the Sange and the Loire, there is a fine view of the whole complex of buildings. Continue on the D951 to Chatillon-sur-Loire, cross the river and return along the north bank as far as **Briare**, famous for its bridge-aqueduct, an original sort of flyover designed by Gustave Eiffel to carry the canal waterway, with its barges and pleasure craft, across the Loire. This watery landscape, criss-crossed by rivers and studded with pools and lakes, is ideal for a quiet walk or fishing expedition. At the southern end of the canal is a marina, where you can hire boats or take a guided tour in a launch. On leaving Briare, take the N7, or the minor roads running parallel to it, to **La Bussière**, which has a small château, rebuilt in the time of Louis XIII, which houses an unusual fishing museum. The water gardens, consisting of the castle moat and an adjoining fish pond, were designed by the famous landscape gardener Le Nôtre. Minor roads lead from here to the D940, and **Gien**.

Gien was at its zenith in the late 15th century, when Anne of Beaujeu, daughter of Louis XI and regent during the early reign of Charles VIII, had a twelve-arched bridge built across the Loire and replaced the old fortress with a magnificent Renaissance château.

From the terrace there is a fine view over the town, the Loire and its valley. Another great tradition of Gien is the manufacture of earthenware, basis of the town's prosperity in the 18th and 19th centuries. The workshops can be visited by appointment.

On leaving Gien, take the D952 as far as Les Bordes, then branch off left to **St-Benoît-sur-Loire**. Just outside this small town, like a ship of stone beside the river, rises the basilica of St-Benoît. The Romanesque building comprises a massive early 11th-century gate-tower, known as the Gauzlin, a late 11th-century choir, transept and crypt, and late 12th-century nave. The harmonious proportions of the whole led the poet Max Jacob to exclaim that 'the Spirit hovers over St-Benoît'! Take time to admire its capitals, sculpted with leaf motifs, animals realistic and fantastic, and scenes from history. Another interesting church, at **Germigny-des-Prés** 5 km north on the D60, rebuilt in the 19th century with materials from the time of Charlemagne, has a 9th-century Byzantine mosaic. Continue to **Châteauneuf-sur-Loire**, self-styled 'centre of merchant shipping on the Loire and of rhododendron growing'. A museum housed in the château has nearly 5,000 exhibits on the history of shipping on the waterway; and its botanical garden is famed for giant rhododendrons set among elms, dogwood and cyprus. Returning to Orléans you can either make a long detour north and west through the vast **Forêt d'Orléans**, perhaps stopping at the Etang de la Vallée near Combreux, or take the shorter N460 via **St-Jean-de-Braye**.

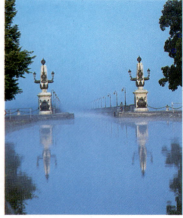

THE BRIDGE-CANAL, BRIARE

THE BERRY

150 km
Map ref.
134 F1

This itinerary explores the Berry region, within the great curve of the Loire. Suggested staging posts are Bourges and St-Amand-Montrond.

Bourges, capital of the Berry, is associated with two larger-than-life personalities: Jean, duke of Berry (1340–1416), famous for his *'Très Riches'* Book of Hours, and Jacques Coeur (1395–1456), finance minister to Charles VII. A recumbent marble statue of Duke Jean lies in the choir of Saint-Etienne's cathedral (near the Tourist Office in rue Victor-Hugo), a fine example of Gothic art, built between 1195 and 1260, which soars above the historic town centre. Graceful flying buttresses uphold the massive bulk of the building, pointing it heavenwards, and seen in profile looking like the motionless oars of an immense stone galley. Clear and stained-glass windows of the 13th, 14th and 15th centuries admit light to the vast interior. The sculptured north and south doors are Romanesque in inspiration; those at the west end, Gothic. The 16th-century north tower has some Renaissance ornamentation.

Leaving the cathedral, head for the picturesque rue Bourbonnaux (via avenue Brisson or the rue des Trois Maillets), with its 15th and 16th-century dwellings. A

THE LOIRE AT GIEN

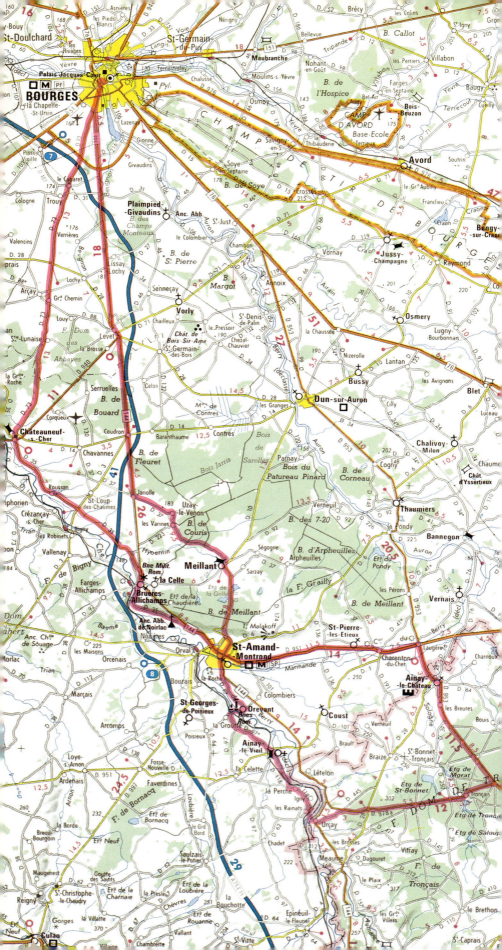

detour to the left brings you to the walkway along the Gallo-Roman ramparts, while the rue de la Thaumassière, to the right, leads to the Musée de l'Ecole, a museum recreating the school environment at the end of the 19th century, with wooden desks and rows of clogs. Also in the rue Bourbonnaux are the Maison des Trois Flûtes and the Hôtel Lallemand, built between 1490 and 1515/1518, with a chapel whose fine coffered ceiling is carved with symbols of the alchemist's art. Nowadays it serves as the Musée des Arts Décoratifs, housing collections of French and Dutch furniture, paintings and tapestries, enamel work and pottery. From the place Gourdaine, take the rue Mirabeau, lined with old houses, where a passageway leads to the rue Branly and the Hôtel des Echevins, a building austere in aspect except for the rich decoration of its octagonal tower. It is now a museum displaying the works of a present-day artist, M. Estève.

Farther along, you come to the rue des Arènes. The 16th-century Hôtel Cujas, a building of ochrous pink stone beneath a blue slate roof, houses the Musée du Berry. In addition to an important archaeological collection and the 16th-century marble statuettes from the tomb of Duc Jean de Berry, the museum has many traditional objects pertaining to the life of the Berry region during the 18th and 19th centuries. Retrace your steps along the rue du Commerce to the rue Jacques Coeur, and the town house of this great merchant, royal banker and adventurer. His medieval palace, built in the middle years of the 15th century, is adorned with Italian embellishments, typifying his luxurious tastes.

Less than 30 km south-west of Bourges, via the D73, is the charming village of **Châteauneuf-sur-Cher**, on the right bank of the river, which here divides into two branches. The Cher, a fisherman's paradise, is not the only attraction: a château commands the valley, and the white basilica of Notre-Dame-des-Enfants, a jewel of religious architecture, points its ornate delicately carved spire skywards. Leave Châteauneuf by the D35 and follow the river to **Noirlac**, famous for its Cistercian abbey, founded by Saint Bernard in 1150. This fine abbey, built during the 12th, 13th and 14th centuries, is a perfect example of the architecture prescribed by this austere monastic order. Centred on the fine cloister, chapter house, dormitories, refectory, storerooms and lay-brothers' quarters have kept their modest grandeur almost intact. From Noirlac, take the N144 five km south-east to **St-Amand-Montrond**, centre of the Boischaut district. The town has an archaeological museum displaying prehistoric and Gallo-Roman remains, and housed in the former town house of the abbots of Noirlac, now the Musée St-Vic. Farther south, along the D97, are the Gallo-Roman ruins of Drévent, an important group of ancient monuments, including theatre and amphitheatre, double baths, forum and temple.

Now branch off the D97, taking the D97E to **Ainay-le-Viel**, known as 'little Carcassonne' on account of its fortified walls. Octagonal in shape, with a tower at each corner and a double-towered gatehouse, the medieval walls conceal an elegant Renaissance dwelling, its delightful stair-tower capped by an unusual inverted-bell-shaped roof. Red-brown tiles alternate with blue-grey slate,

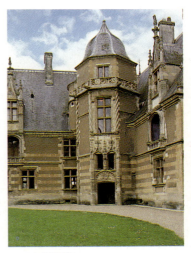

MEILLANT CHATEAU

and the pale ochre of the building stone reminds us that we are on the border between the Loire and the Auvergne regions. At the foot of the château is a superb rose garden, with varieties dating back as far as 1420!

Our next stage is through the Forest of Tronçay or Tronçais on the D118, D445, D978, to enjoy some fine natural scenery. (If you stop for a walk in this forest, a haunt of red deer and wild boar, you will find mature oaks of majestic proportions. In spring and summer the woods are alive with butterflies; in autumn mushrooms abound. For nature lovers, this is the perfect spot for a stroll.) You can swim and practise watersports at the St-Bonnet lake, and there is *gîte* accommodation nearby. Leave the forest by the D953, turn left on to the D951 at Ainay-le-Château, and so back to St-Amand-Montrond, where you take the D10 to **Meillant**. This château is a mixture of High Gothic and Renaissance styles, with a sumptuous chapel and hexagonal tower, created by the Italian architect Fra Giocondo.

To return to Bourges, 35 km north of Meillant, take the D10, D37 and finally the N144.

WALKS

This chapter suggests some walks in different parts of the Loire valley and adjoining areas. They are all circular tours and generally follow established waymarked paths (*Grande Randonnée* routes) from village to village, exploring areas of unspoilt scenery. For further information on existing paths, or to obtain detailed guides to particular *départements*, apply to the tourist offices at Angers, Tours, Orléans, Châteauroux and Bourges. All the maps in this section are 1:25,000 unless otherwise indicated. In order to pinpoint the start of each walk, a map reference has been provided relating to the atlas.

IN THE VALLEY OF THE INDRE

16 km
Map ref.
138 B3

A tour of village churches and chapels between Palluau-sur-Indre and Le Tranger, and the Château de la Mardelle. The village of **Palluau-sur-Indre** is well worth a visit before you start the walk. St-Sulpice, a former collegiate foundation, dates from the 12th and 14th centuries, while the old church of St-Laurent contains some fine Romanesque frescoes. The château is part of a fortress built in the 11th century by Foulques de Rechin, count of Anjou. A double medieval wall surrounds the keep, a chapel decorated with frescoes and living quarters built in the Gothic style but furnished à la Renaissance. From the tower there is an outstanding view over the valley of the Indre.

On leaving Palluau, take the waymarked GR46 along the Indre valley. The river flows through a landscape of hedges, meadows and poplar plantations, with hamlets and several minor châteaux dotted here and there in the gentle folds of the countryside.

Between Palluau and Le Tranger, a 250-metre detour to your left will bring you to the chapel of Bonne Nouvelle. The path then follows the edge of the Bois du Tranger, before entering the village itself. From the heights to the north of Le Tranger, you can make out the Château de L'île Savary, built in the 15th century on an island in the Indre by Guillaume de Varye, a financier in the service of Jacques Coeur.

If you wish to press on to the Château de la Mardelle, follow the GR46, passing close to Semblançay, and turn off right 500 metres beyond the village, following the signs to La Mardelle and La Bouchoire.

For the return, you can retrace your steps via the GR46, or go by minor tarmac roads, passing through the hamlets of **La Bouchoire**, **Le Grand Villiers**, **Le Bas Village** and close to the Château de Paray, and so back to **Palluau**.

🛈 Syndicat d'Initiative, place Fontenac, Palluau-sur-Indre ☎ 54.38.53.03.

THE INDRE VALLEY

WALKS

IN THE VALLEY OF THE CHER

8.5 km
Map ref. 131 C4

FOOTPATH IN SOLOGNE

The focal point of this itinerary is Monthou-sur-Cher, a village set amid vineyards and woodland, not far to the north of the Cher. The route runs through varied scenery, taking in the Château de Gué-Péan and the Moulin du Ru. You will be walking the GR41, waymarked in red and white, except between Monthou and the château, where the paths are waymarked in yellow.

Take the D21 north out of **Monthou**, pass through **La Varenne** and turn left when you come to a fork 100 metres farther on. Soon after reaching the edge of the woods, you will join the path which circles the château. After the ruins of 'La Rodière' farm, the path enters an area of brushwood. Out in the open again, cross the Bavet stream and turn right. You are now in the vicinity of two lakes: the Etang de l'Ermitage and the Etang de Brault. Carry straight on for 500 metres, until you come to the wide private driveway of the Château de Gué-Péan, on your right. About 100 metres down the driveway you encounter another area of brushwood, before emerging at the stables of Le Gué-Péan. The château itself, built in the 16th and 17th centuries, is Renaissance in conception: a rectangular structure flanked by four large round towers, but the façades giving onto the inner courtyard are of classical inspiration. Surrounded by a dry moat, it seems to rest on a bed of green at the edge of the forest of Choussy. Three of the towers are surmounted by pepper-pot turrets, while the fourth is crowned with a massive slate-roofed dome and lantern. Inside the château are treasures both historical and artistic: a monumental fireplace by the great sculptor Germain Pilon; Louis XII's bed and La Fayette's writing desk; paintings by Guido, Fragonard and Caravaggio; modern works by Dali, Carzou and Klein; letters bearing the signatures of Victor Hugo, Marcel Proust and Mauriac.

From the entrance to the château park, you turn left and follow the right-hand side of the tree-lined avenue until you come to a path on your right, which crosses the Bavet. From this vantage point, there is a good view back to the château. A little further on, rejoin the pathway you came by, and so return to **Monthou**.
Starting out again from the village, go straight from the Mairie to the 'Villa Ariane'

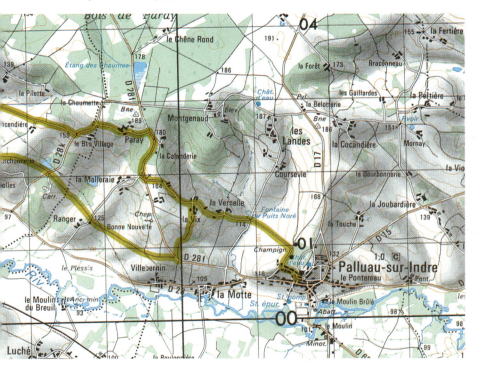

and join the GR41. When you come to a large boulder, 1,500 metres farther on, turn right. The path then crosses the Thésée road and leads down through a delightful pattern of vineyards. Fifty metres before you reach the Cher, at **Les Maselles**, are the Gallo-Roman ruins of Thésée, formerly Tasciaca. Surrounded by a rampart, the buildings date from the 2nd century AD, and are in an exceptional state of preservation. Only a short detour away is the modern village of **Thésée**, where artefacts found on the site can be viewed in the archaeological museum.

From Les Maselles, the GR41 continues to the bank of the Cher. Yellow waymarks indicate the pathway along the river bank, which passes in the vicinity of the Moulin du Ru. Near Arche Mace, branch off right to La Verrerie, and rejoin the GR41 which leads back through vineyards to **Monthou**.

TWO WALKS IN THE SOLOGNE
AROUND LIGNY-LE-RIBAULT

19 km
Map ref.
122 E3

Most of this circular walk is waymarked with orange batons. The final stretch, from Ligny-le-Ribault to the Château de Bon Hôtel and back, is not waymarked, but the way is not difficult to find.

Leave **Ligny-le-Ribault** by the D61 towards La Ferté-St-Aubin and branch off left on to a narrow tarmac road which runs through a housing development, then becomes a track through woodland. The pathway skirts the Château de la Bretèche, passing through gently undulating country, then through marshy woodland and past ancient oak trees. You rejoin the D61 close by a farm with timber-frame and brickwork buildings. Follow the road briefly, as far as the Château de la Frogerie, then, leaving the château on your left, turn right in the direction indicated by the 'Villeneuve-la-Margerie' sign. The path cuts through woods, past the hamlet of Les Bordes, then skirts a dried marsh with reed-beds frequented by marshland birds.

At the next crossways, you will see the Château de la Touche on your left and in front of you the Etang de la Rosa. Take the path to the right, the GR3C, which leads back to **Ligny** via **La Couvrée** – a spot surrounded by ponds – and the château of Vieux Maisons. From the path branching off left to the château, you can make a detour to the right and visit the interesting brickworks of la Bretèche. On reaching Ligny, take the D61 left and follow the road until you come to the village. On your right you will find a road leading to the majestic Château de Bon Hôtel, built in the 19th century and clearly modelled on Chambord. Behind the château, turn right on to the road back to **Ligny**.

WALKS 57

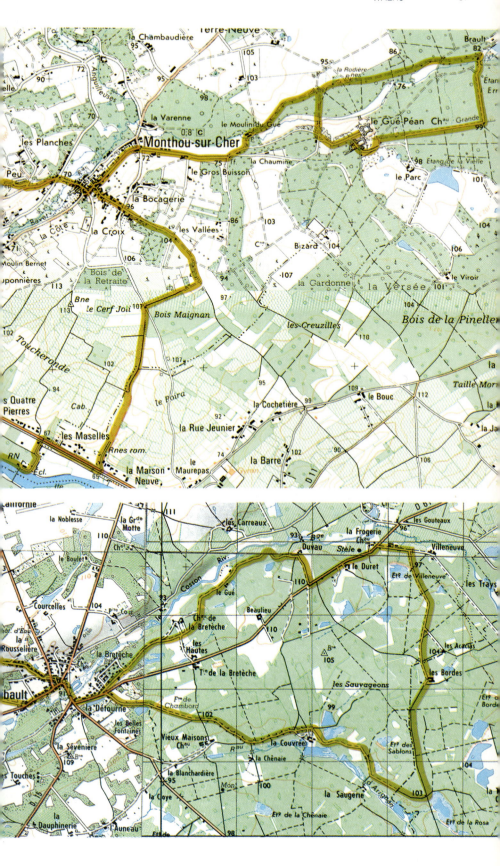

AROUND MENESTREAU-EN-VILLETTE

17 km
Map ref.
123 E4

Waymarked in brown, this walk takes you to an estate described as a 'living museum' of the Sologne's life and landscape.

Starting from the centre of **Ménestreau** village, head along beside the church towards the Mairie and take the road to **Moinard**. Leave the tarmac road when you come to the farm of Courcelle, taking a track which first crosses open land, then plunges into the forest of La Motte Beuvron. At the Chambouy crossroads, take the path on the extreme right, the GR3 trail from Gien to Chambord, which shortly after crosses a tarmac road. Continue on the same path until you pass the boundary of La Cantarelle and reach the Etang du Donjon, a listed site rich in wildlife. Turn left at this point and take the path between this lake and the Etang du Briou. Farther on you reach the tarmac road to La Ferté-St-Aubin. Follow it to the left for several hundred metres, as far as Maisoncelle, where you rejoin the path (on your right). Go on to la Tabardière, where you leave the waymarked route, and continue straight on to the Château

MUSEUM OF SOLOGNE

du Masuray and then to the crossroads known as 'Les Quatre Routes'. Here take the D108, to the left, for 350 metres, then turn left again, which will bring you to the Domaine du Ciran.

This property, comprising 300 hectares or 740 acres of woodland, meadow, heath and ponds is owned by the Fondation Sologne and under their management has become a living museum of the Sologne countryside. There sleeping accommodation and camping facilities are available in a natural setting. The château itself houses a permanent exhibition of the crafts and traditions of the Sologne and its unique environment. On leaving the domaine, retrace your steps to the crossroads and turn right towards **Le Masuray**, then right again. The path passes the Etang du Menil then the Etang Communal. Here you will find brown waymarks again, leading back to **Ménestreau-en-Villette**.

WALKS

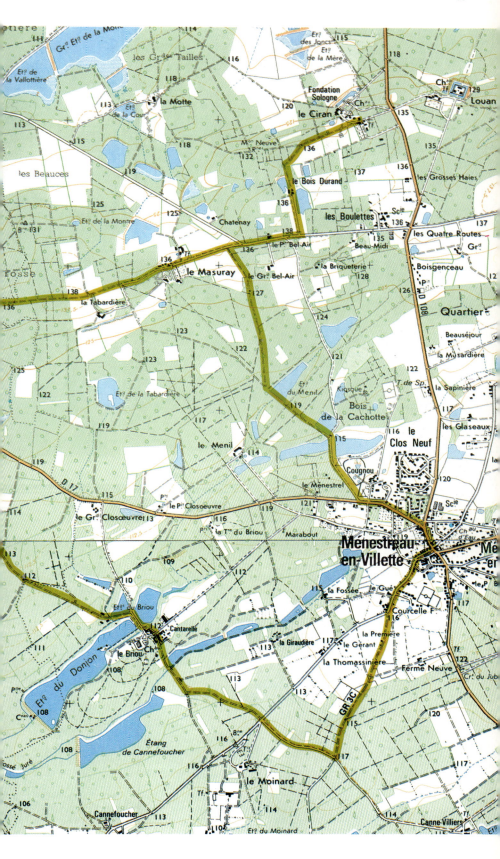

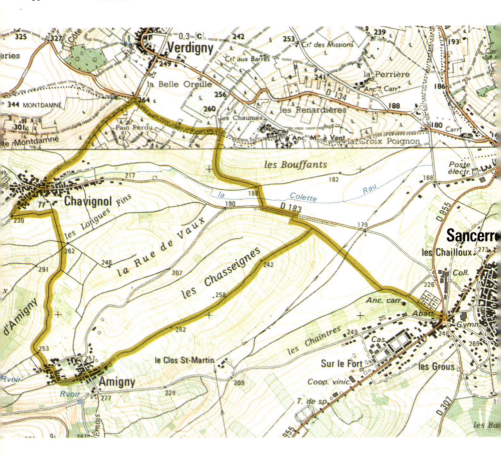

IN THE 'SANCERROIS'

12 km
Map ref.
135 C4

A walk through the farmland around Sancerre, Chavignol and Amigny.

The small town of **Sancerre**, our starting point, is the ancient capital of the Comté district. Narrow streets lead to the old town, perched on top of a hill. Here you will find the 12th-century Tour des Fiefs, the château, and turreted and gabled 15th-century houses. From the Porte de César there is a breathtaking view over vineyards, the village of St-Satur and the valley of the Loire.

As you leave the town in a south-westerly direction, you will pick up the waymarks of the GR31 to the right of the crossroads, between the D7 and the D955. Follow the footpath, cross the D183, and continue westwards towards Chavignol. From the high ground you will have a view of vineyards and, occasionally, brown goats with black muzzles grazing on the thin grass of the meadows. **Chavignol**, a small village whose inhabitants make their living by producing wine, also has a reputation for making goat's cheese, known as 'Crottin de Chavignol'.

From Chavignol, follow the waymarked path due south towards **Amigny**, a pretty village, where you will also find wine cellars and goat's cheese for sale. Leaving the village, the path runs north-eastwards and intersects the D183. Here you turn right, and go back to **Sancerre** by the same route as you took on the way out. Back in town after your exertions, you might try the local white wine: dry, fruity, slightly acidic with a touch of mellowness. With some of the local goat's cheese and a few walnuts to line your stomach, it should not have too powerful an effect!

THE SANCERROIS VINEYARDS

BICYCLE RIDES

ON THE COTEAUX DU LAYON

19 km
Map ref.
126 C1

A riverside ride from L'île-Béhuard to St-Aubin-de-Luigné, via Rochefort-sur-Loire and the Chaudefonds vineyards. **Béhuard** is a curious village, sited as it is on an island in the middle of the Loire. In the days when the river was still an important artery for commercial shipping, it served as a landmark for boatmen. It had a shrine originally consecrated to some goddess of the sea, who in time relinquished her throne to the Virgin Mary. Louis XI, who narrowly escaped drowning at this spot, had a new place of worship built there in the years between 1462 and 1472. You can still visit this modest church, half carved out of the rock, where the Virgin of Béhuard, richly dressed in brocades, reigns over the waters. Louis himself is supposed to have stayed at the 15th-century house opposite.
Head west out of the village, cross the

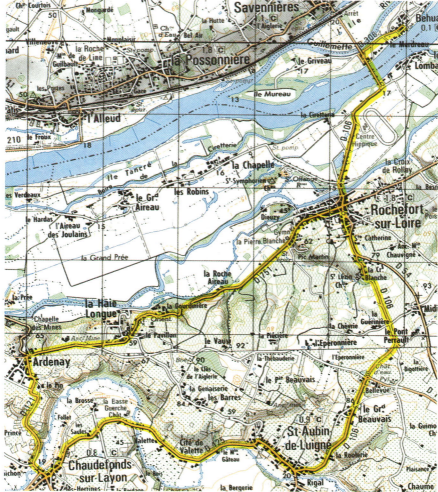

NOHANT CHATEAU

Loire on the right and travel along beside the race course until you reach the bank of the Louet. Before you come to **Rochefort-sur-Loire**, you can make a short detour to see the Château de St-Offrange. From the village of Rochefort, take the D751 along the Corniche Angevine, a scenic road running parallel with the river, which here borders on marshland as far as La Haie Longue. Continue to **Ardenay**, then branch off southwards on minor roads to **Chaudefonds-sur-Layon**, set amid vineyards. From Chaudefonds, the road to **St-Aubin-de-Luigné** passes close to the manor of La Basse-Guerche, on the banks of the Layon, and then the 15th-century Château de la Haute-Guerche. You can stop at St-Aubin to go boating on the river, before returning to Rochefort-sur-Loire via the D106. From Rochefort back to **Béhuard**, take the same route as on the outward journey.

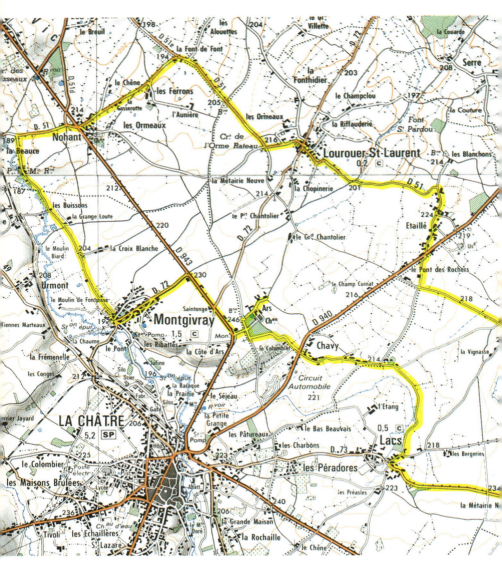

BICYCLE RIDES

IN THE BOISCHAUT: GEORGE SAND COUNTRY

33 km
Map ref. 140 E2

La Châtre is at the heart of the country associated with George Sand, the 19th-century romantic novelist. She called this little-known, mysterious region the 'Vallée Noire' or black valley because of the violet-coloured sky effected by the blue of the Marche mountains and the dark woods which cover them. The Mairie of Montgivray, where this tour begins, was formerly the home of her daughter. Surrounded by a park, the rustic, ivy-mantled building stands facing a Roman bridge.

From **Montgivray**, where the 12th-century village church is decorated with sculptured figures dating from the time of its foundation, take first the D72 then the D943 to the Château d'Ars. Along the route there are some fine views over the valley. Approaching Ars, branch off right on the minor road to **Chavy** and on to **Lacs**, whose 12th-century Romanesque church houses a fragment of a Gallo-Roman altar. Carry on through the village and continue south-east as far as **Montlevicq**, a little village with a 15th-century château and 12th-century church. At this point you are not far from the course of the Igneraie which runs parallel with the road as far as **Priches**. From Priches, turn north to **Fontenay** and join the D68, which will bring you back to the banks of the Igneraie at **Cosnay**, another village boasting its own small château and an old chapel.

Continue north-westwards to **Lourouer-St-Laurent**, where the choir of the 12th-century church is decorated with wall paintings and wooden panelling. Farther on in the same direction is the Château de Nohant, the house in which George Sand herself lived. Today the 18th-century château is a museum, where relics of this exceptional woman have been religiously preserved, and echoes of former 'Romantic' gatherings are still very much in the air.

A minor road running alongside the Indre to **Montgivray** completes the tour.

GEORGE SAND'S PIANO

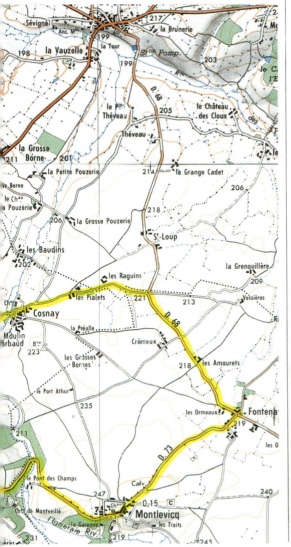

NOHANT

GAZETTEER

The Loire valley, with its associated wealth of châteaux, cathedrals and world-famous vineyards properly belongs to that region of France known as Centre – Val de Loire, which is divided administratively into six *départements*, the rough equivalent of British counties, and named: Cher, Eure-et-Loir, Indre, Indre-et-Loire, Loir-et-Cher and Loiret.

The A-Z gazetteer section which follows features a selection of the region's top locations, be they sleepy rural villages of great charm or major centres for shopping and cultural excursions. Each entry contains details on who to contact for sports and activity pursuits, and numerous other suggestions are listed to add to the enjoyment of your stay. Selected hotels, campsites and restaurants are included, and a host of facts of historical, architectural and general interest to complete your appreciation of this great holiday region.

In fact, all your questions are answered on what to do, what to see and where to go.

LEFT AZAY-LE-RIDEAU CHATEAU
ABOVE CAVE DWELLINGS NEAR PARNAY

AMBOISE
Map ref. 130 C2
Pop 12,000
Tours 25 km
Blois 35 km
Orléans 95 km
Paris 220 km
🛈 quai Général-de-Gaulle
☎ 47.57.09.28

The late 15th-century château, set high above the Loire on a terraced spur, commands a magnificent view over the town and valley. During July and August a *son-et-lumière* spectacle is held, recalling the period when François I and his court were established here. For their entertainment were staged a succession of brilliant festivals and balls, tournaments and wild beast fights. Having purchased the *Mona Lisa*, the king then established its artist, Leonardo da Vinci, at Amboise, where he continued to work until his death. Not far away is the lovely **Château de Chenonceau**, astride the River Cher. As the home of Henri II's beautiful mistress Diane de Poitiers, fine gardens were laid down and a bridge thrown across between château and riverbank. When Henry died, killed in a duel, his wife Catherine de Médicis compelled Diane to surrender her beloved Chenonceau, and further gardens and parkland were planned, together with the construction of a gallery to the bridge. From May to September *son-et-lumière* is staged and throughout this area there are numerous caves or cellars offering wine-tasting.

Leisure
Art Leonardo, artist, sculptor, architect and engineer, spent his last years at Amboise. In the basement of the Manoir de Clos-Lucé there is an exhibition of scale models of machines based on his amazingly scientific and prophetic drawings.
Boat Trips When the water level permits, there are trips on the Cher, and helicopter trips depart from Neuvy-le-Roi to take visitors over the area ☎ 47.24.81.44
Château Château d'Amboise open daily, all year ☎ 47.57.00.98 and Château de Chenonceau open daily, all year ☎ 47.23.90.07
Cycling Cycles for hire from the SNCF station.
Festival Each summer, Jul-Aug, a re-creation of the history of the royal Château d'Amboise is staged by hundreds of local people with elaborate costumes, fireworks and period music.
Wine Tastings and cellar tours at Cave Girault-Artois, 7 quai des Violettes ☎ 47.57.07.71

Hotels
Hostellerie le Choiseul ★★★★
36 quai Guinot
☎ 47.30.45.45
(and restaurant)
Le Chanteloup ★★★
avenue de Bléré
☎ 47.57.10.90
Novotel Amboise ★★★
rue des Sablonnières
route de Chenonceaux
☎ 47.57.42.07
(and restaurant)
Château de Pray ★★★
N751, 2 km north
☎ 47.57.23.67
(and restaurant)
Le Parc ★★★
8 avenue Léonard de Vinci
☎ 47.57.06.93
Le Lion d'Or ★★
quai Guinot
☎ 47.57.00.23
(and restaurant)

Camping
Municipal de l'Ile d'Or ★★
☎ 47.57.23.23
520 places

Restaurant
Le Manoir Saint-Thomas ★★★★
mail Saint-Thomas
☎ 47.57.22.52

LEONARDO DA VINCI (1452-1519)
It was in keeping with his reputation as the perfect Renaissance prince and patron of the arts that François I should invite Leonardo da Vinci in 1516 to live near his château at Amboise. Leonardo stayed as the king's guest until his death at the age of 67, three years later, dying apparently in the king's arms. The *Mona Lisa*, brought with him from Italy, hung in the château and still remains today in France, occupying pride of place in the Louvre.

Da Vinci's period at Amboise is commemorated by an exhibition in the basement of the manor at Clos-Lucé dedicated to his life's work as painter, poet, architect, engineer and scholar, and where fifty scale models based on his extraordinarily prophetic drawings can be seen.

GAZETTEER

SLIPPING OVER THE BORDER *into Pays de la Loire*

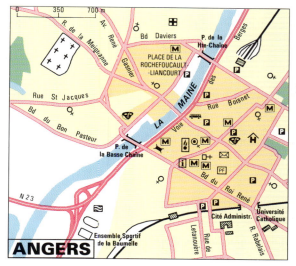

ANGERS
Map ref. 130 C2
Pop 210,000
Tours 108 km
Blois 154 km
Orléans 211 km
Paris 292 km
🛈 place Kennedy
☎ 41.88.69.93
🛈 place de la Gare
☎ 41.87.72.50

An elegant city rich in museums and treasures, Angers stands on the River Maine, the seventeen-towered military fortress built around 1230, first to dominate the Loire valley and in later centuries converted to more domestic use as royal apartments for the dukes of Anjou and their court. Today the magnificent 14th-century tapestry, *l'Apocalypse*, stretching over 102 m and in seventy-two pieces, is housed within the château. Sustaining its reputation for work in this medium, the city has created and developed a Regional Centre for Textile Art and a gallery of contemporary work can also be visited.

This is also the city of the famous liqueur, Cointreau, and of the Angevin wines, its vineyards extending principally to the south of the Loire and east towards Saumur. Red, white and rosé wines are produced and you can follow the *Route du Vin* trail of vineyards and *dégustations* or tastings to discover and celebrate them for yourself.'Dis-moi si ton vin est gai que je me réjouisse avec toi!' as the saying goes.

With all the cultural attractions of a large city, Angers is an ideal base from which to visit the châteaux of Anjou, or to enjoy the fishing and varied watersports facilities offered on the Lac de Maine only five minutes out of the city. For those moving on and wishing to pursue different themes of the region's heritage, three motorists' touring routes can be followed: the *Route Roi René*, the *Route des Plantagenêts* and the *Route Vendée Militaire*, details of which can be obtained from the Tourist Office.

Leisure
Art Paintings in the Musée des Beaux Arts, rue du Musée; sculptures in the Galerie David d'Angers, rue Toussaint; and

Hotels
Altéa – Lac de Maine ★★★
route de Nantes
☎ 41.48.02.12
Anjou ★★★
1 boulevard Foch
☎ 41.88.24.82
Concorde ★★★
18 boulevard Foch
☎ 41.87.37.20
France ★★★
8 place de la Gare
☎ 41.88.49.42
Mercure ★★★
1 place Mendès-France
☎ 41.60.34.81
Progrès ★★★
26 rue Dénis-Papin
☎ 41.88.10.14
Boule d'Or ★★
27 boulevard Carnot
☎ 41.43.76.56

Camping
Lac de Maine ★★★
☎ 41.73.05.03
160 places, open all year

Youth Hostel
Centre d'Accueil du
Lac de Maine
route de Pruniers
open all year
☎ 41.48.57.01

Restaurants
La Rose d'Anjou ★★★
9 place du Ralliement
☎ 41.87.64.94
Le Toussaint ★★★
place Kennedy
☎ 41.87.46.20
Le Vert d'Eau ★★★
boulevard Gaston-Dumesnil
☎ 41.48.52.31

ANGERS CHATEAU

contemporary works in tapestry are shown at Musée Jean Lurçat, boulevard Arago which also houses Lurçat's impressive Le Chant du Monde.
Ballooning Apr-Oct, min. six passengers. Enquire at the Tourist Office.
Boat Hire Cabin cruisers to hire here and at Grez-Neuville.
Boat Trips Daily dine-and-cruise river trips operate from quai de la Savatte, Mar-Nov.
Château In the promenade du Bout du Monde, open all year ☎ 41.87.43.47
Cycling Cycles can be hired from the SNCF station.
Gardens The city boasts many open spaces and gardens, notable amongst them being the botanical garden, Jardin des Plantes and the arboretum, Gaston Allard.
Golf 18-hole private course at Golf d'Angers, Moulin de Pistrait, St-Jean-des-Mauvrets, 49320 Brissac Quince ☎ 41.91.96.56
Guided Tours Walking tours of the city and guided tours aboard a little tourist train are bookable from the Tourist Office.
Watersports Swimming, sailing, pedalos, etc at the Parc de Loisirs du Lac de Maine ☎ 41.48.12.47, open all year.
Wine The Maison de Vin de l'Anjou, place Kennedy ☎ 41.88.81.13 closed Mon, will both enlighten and provide literature on the motoring Route du Vin; and the Espace Cointreau, carrefour Molière, St-Barthélemy, open all year, offers guided visits.

ARGENTON-SUR-CREUSE
Map ref. 139 F4
Pop 6,000
Châteauroux 32 km
Tours 128 km
Blois 133 km
Orléans 173 km
Paris 297 km
🛈 Ancien Hôtel de Scévole
☎ 54.24.05.30

The pretty, galleried houses which line and overhang the curving river are frequently photographed by passing tourists, travelling on the major through routes in the direction of Limoges, Poitiers, Bourges or Tours. Six Roman roads converged at this point, an indication of the strategic importance that 'Argentomagus' once held. Substantial Roman remains and artefacts are displayed at **St-Marcel**, 2 km north. Though the Paris-Toulouse traffic is now carried on a new viaduct, the medieval bridge still spans the river, the watermills continue to turn and the ancient houses and narrow streets of the old town lead up to an impressive bronze statue of the

Hotels
Central Hôtel **
☎ 54.24.41.01
(and restaurant)
Hôtel du Cheval Noir **
27 rue Auclert-Descottes
☎ 54.24.00.06
(and restaurant)

Camping
Municipal les Chambons ***
☎ 54.24.15.26
85 places
Camping de Chambon **
☎ 54.47.44.85
100 places

Restaurants
Chez Maitre Jean *
avenue Rollinat
☎ 54.01.18.72
Rive Droite *
rue Ledru-Rollin
☎ 54.24.01.06

THE BLACK VALLEY OF THE CREUSE NEAR ARGENTIN

Virgin. Over 6 m high, 'La Bonne Dame' commands and dominates the town below. Though only 100 years old herself, she stands at the entrance to the chapel of St-Benoît in which there is a stone carved Virgin which dates from 1485 and which is the focus of an important annual pilgrimage each September.

South of Argenton, and leading towards the dammed-off section which has created Lac Chambon, the gorges of the Creuse valley can be followed, in parts quite closely. The little village of **Gargilesse** is especially worth visiting and local specialities of this country area include honey and goats' cheese.

Leisure
Fishing Category 2 fishing on the River Creuse.
Golf 18-hole course at Golf Club des Dryades, Pouligny-Notre-Dame, 36160 Sainte-Sévère-sur-Indre ☎ 54.30.28.00
Watersports Lac Chambon, 20 km south, has beaches at Eguzon and sailing, water-skiing, pedalo hire and other facilities.

AUBIGNY

AUBIGNY-SUR-NERE
Map ref. 134 B1
Pop 6,000
Orléans 69 km
Paris 180 km
🛈 rue des Dames
☎ 48.58.00.09

In the mid-15th century, and as a reward for coming to the aid of Charles VII in his fight against the English, this small town was given to the Scot, John Stuart of Darnley. From this date Aubigny came under the influence and control of the Stuart dynasty, the present-day Hôtel de Ville being the family's château. On the well-known *Jacques-Coeur* château route for motorists and with the major châteaux of the Loire 90 km away, this tranquil and pretty little town of half-timbered houses, and the area which surrounds it, is a delight for walkers, artists or cyclists. Also on the *Route Jacques-Coeur* is the elegant **Château de la Verrerie** in a beautiful lakeside and woodland setting. Built at the beginning of the Renaissance period by the Stuarts, it was later to be inherited by Louise de Kéroualle, Duchess of Portsmouth and mistress of the English monarch, Charles II. She lived there for some time as did her sons, the Dukes of Richmond, after her.
The largest artificial lake in the Sologne region, the Etang de Puits, situated 12 km

Hotels
Hôtel la Chaumière ✶✶
place Paul-Lasnier
☎ 48.58.04.01
(and restaurant)
Hôtel la Fontaine ✶✶
2 avenue du Général-Leclerc
☎ 48.58.34.41
Hôtel le Sulky ✶✶
135 av. de l'Hippodrome
☎ 48.58.33.50

Camping
Camping Fédéral du Parc des Sports ✶✶
☎ 48.58.02.37
100 places

Youth Hostel
Parc des Sports
☎ 48.24.58.09
May-Oct

ALAIN FOURNIER (1886-1914)

Alain Fournier, christened Henri Alban, was born in the tiny village of La Chapelle-d'Angillon in the Cher. Killed in action on the Meuse at the age of 27, his writing career was brief but was marked by the publication of Le Grand Meaulnes in 1913, one of the greatest novels of the twentieth century.

The story of a young man lost in an evocatively and nostalgically beautiful world in which the perfect Yvonne de Galais lives, it is based on Fournier's own love for the original Yvonne whom he met while working in Paris. The misty atmosphere of the novel is essentially that of the Berry countryside he knew so well.

The old school in the little village of Epineul-le-Fleuriel, due south of St-Amand-Montrond, where the author was a pupil, has now been turned into a Fournier museum and can be visited on Wednesdays and Sundays, or by appointment ☎ 48.63.02.23. A museum to his memory is situated in the Château de la Chapelle-d'Angillon, known as La Béthune, and very probably the model for the novel's own Domaine des Sablières, though it is also suggested that the Château de la Verrerie is a possibility. La Chapelle-d'Angillon is north of Bourges, 14 km south of Aubigny-sur-Nère, and is open daily, except Sun ☎ 48.73.41.10.

north of the town, is a popular base for the practice of most watersports and for fishing.

Leisure
Château Attractively furnished and set deep within woodland, La Verrerie is open daily, Mar-Dec.
Cycling Cycles available for hire from the campsite.
Fishing Category 1 fishing on the Nère river and on the Etang de Puits.
Golf See Romorantin-Lanthenay, Sancerre and Sully-sur-Loire.
Riding Relais Equestre Les Grands at Argent-sur-Sauldre ☎ 48.73.64.19

Restaurants
Les Charmilles **
6 rue du Château
☎ 48.58.17.18
Auberge de la Fontaine **
avenue Charles-de-Gaulle
☎ 48.58.02.59

AZAY-LE-RIDEAU
Map ref. 128 D3
Pop 3,000
Chinon 21 km
Tours 26 km
Blois 86 km
Orléans 143 km
Paris 254 km
🛈 42 rue Nationale
☎ 47.45.44.40

One of the essential château visits and en route for those of Langeais and Villandry both 10 km away, the feminine elegance of Azay, its walls dipping into the moated waters of the Indre, will not fail to charm. Its small scale and decorative grace may surprise, but this was not a château built as a fortification like its close neighbour Chinon. Constructed in the early 16th century on earlier ruins, and on the instructions of the Master of the King's Purse, Gilles Berthelot, it is his wife's influence which can be felt in its planning. Confiscated by the crown shortly afterwards, it has changed hands frequently and since 1905 has been state-owned. The interior has been arranged as a Renaissance museum with period style

Hotels
Hostellerie du Château de Montgoger ***
St-Epain
☎ 47.65.54.22
(and restaurant)
Hôtel le Grand Monarque **
place de la République
☎ 47.45.40.08
(and restaurant)
Les Trois Lys **
2 rue du Château
☎ 47.45.40.73
(and restaurant)

Camping
Municipal le Camp du Château **
☎ 47.45.42.72
50 places

Restaurants
L'Aigle d'Or
avenue A.-Riché
☎ 47.45.24.58
Les Grottes
rue Pineau
☎ 47.45.21.04

AZAY-LE-RIDEAU

tapestries and furniture but it is its external appearance and features such as the grand staircase and its superb setting amidst shaded parkland and lawns that most impress.

Also in the area are the novelist Balzac's château home in the little village of **Saché**, 8 km away and staging summertime *son-et-lumière* productions, and the troglodyte houses at **Villaines-les-Rochers**, 5 km distant, where craftsmen produce basketwork.

Leisure
Château Open daily in season with *son-et-lumière performances regularly staged*, May-Sep ☎ 47.45.42.04
Cycling Cycles for hire from the SNCF station.
Fishing Category 2 fishing on the Indre.
Golf See Chinon.
Wine Tastings and cellar tours at Château de l'Aulée, route de Tours ☎ 47.45.40.58

THE NUCLEAR POWER STATION AT BELLEVILLE

THE LOIRE IN THE NUCLEAR AGE

As with conventional power stations which use oil or coal, nuclear power stations transform energy liberated by combustion, in the form of heat. The Loire power stations operate on two different systems the UNGG (*uranium naturel-graphite-gaz*) system was the first to be used. Its fuel is natural uranium; graphite contributes a moderating role, slowing the neutrons (slow neutrons create greater fission than rapid ones), while the carbon gas is the transport medium, carrying the heat released by fission, in the form of water vapour, to a turbine which operates an alternator to produce electricity. However, units equipped with this system are being closed down in favour of a second system – the PWR (pressurized water reactor) which is fuelled by enriched uranium, with ordinary water acting as the transport medium, and pressurized water as moderator.

The Loire has four nuclear power stations at Belleville upstream from Gien and at Dampierre between Gien and Sully-sur-Loire (both PWR), and also at St-Laurent-des-Eaux between Beaugency and Blois and at Avoine near Chinon, the oldest in France (both UNGG and PWR).

Standing on the banks of the Loire at the heart of the Chinon area, the Avoine power station is unmistakeable with its immense cooling towers crowned with steam, and vast metallic sphere where production is now halted. Open to the public, this spherical building still retains its complex and impressive production machinery in working order.

The St-Laurent-des-Eaux power station, built on an artificial island in one of the loops of the river, has an information centre on the edge of the site, where models, photographs, plans, and audiovisual displays introduce visitors to the complexities of this most modern of technologies.

BEAUGENCY

Map ref. 122 D2
Pop 8,000
Orléans 30 km
Chateauroux 59 km
Tours 100 km
Blois 124 km
Paris 140 km
🛈 place du Martroi
☎ 38.44.54.42

The great twenty-two-arched medieval bridge spans the Loire here, dominated by the ancient fortified town of narrow streets. Built in the 15th century for Joan of Arc's companion, Jean Dunois, the Château de Dunois, with a fine original 11th-century keep, today houses an interesting 'museum of everyday life', each room being devoted to a particular theme. The Hôtel de Ville contains some wonderful 17th-century embroidered hangings, still richly coloured.

From this picturesque setting, the town is an excellent base for touring east of Blois, with a first stop perhaps at the fortress château of **Meung-sur-Loire**. Originally dating from the 12th century, and longtime residence of the Bishops of Orléans, it became an important prison during the medieval period and is renowned for its dungeons and *oubliettes*, grim places where prisoners were left and literally forgotten.

Alternatively, and as something of a dramatic contrast, the nuclear power station at St-Laurent-des-Eaux, whose riverside installation dominates the landscape south of Beaugency, is also open to visitors.

Hotels
Hôtel Abbaye ✱✱✱
quai de l'Abbaye
☎ 38.44.67.35
(and restaurant)
Hôtel Ecu de Bretagne ✱✱
place du Martroi
☎ 38.44.67.60
(and restaurant)
Hôtel du Mail ✱✱
4 rue du Puits Manu
☎ 38.44.53.30
Hôtel Relais des Templiers ✱✱
rue du Pont
☎ 38.43.53.78

Camping
Municipal ✱✱
☎ 38.44.50.39
400 places

Youth Hostel
Hameau de Vernon
route de Châteaudun
☎ 38.44.61.31
Apr-Nov

BEAUGENCY CHATEAU

Leisure
Château The Château de Meung-sur-Loire is open daily, Easter-Nov ☎ 38.44.36.47
Cycling Cycles for hire from the SNCF station.
Fishing Category 2 fishing on the Loire.
Golf 18-hole private course at Golf International les Bordes, Saint-Laurent-Nouan, 41220 La Ferté-Saint-Cyr ☎ 54.87.72.13; and long 18-hole private course at Golf Club de Sologne, Country Club des Olleries, route de Jouy-le-Potier, 45160 La Ferté-Saint-Aubin ☎ 38.76.57.33; see also Orléans.
Loisirs Accueil Thirteen-day kayaking and cycling holiday combined: five days spent cycling from Beaugency to Chaumont through the Sologne and château country,

followed by a five-day camping and paddling trip down the Loire returning to Beaugency for three days in the Youth Hostel. From sixteen yrs upwards, price is 3,100FF per person, Jul-Aug, and includes equipment, accommodation and supervisor for both sections of the trip. Details from Loisirs Accueil Loiret (address on page 27).

Museum Musée des Arts et Traditions has a collection which includes furniture, costumes, dolls, medieval sculpture and a display telling the story of the bridges which cross the Loire. Open all year, closed Tues.

Nuclear Power Station Explanatory information centre and viewing tower open daily. Visits to the interior of the installation are made in groups, by prior written appointment only, though individuals may be able to join a group where space allows and by prior telephone appointment. Foreign visitors must present their passports. Contact Electricité de France, Centre de Production Nucléaire de St-Laurent-des-Eaux, Relations Publiques, BP 42, St-Laurent-Nouan, 41220 La Ferté-St-Cyr ☎ 54.44.84.08

LE BLANC
Map ref. 138 E1
Pop 8,000
Châteauroux 60 km
Paris 300 km
🛈 10, rue Collin-de-Souvigny
☎ 54.37.05.13
Summer only

Crossed by the winding Creuse river and built on both sides of the valley, this pleasant little town's origins pre-date even its period of Roman occupation when its name was 'Oblincum'. According to legend, this was the scene of the massacre of the four 'Bons Saints du Blanc' in the 4th century, an incident recalled annually on the first Sunday in September. From the 12th-century château in the terraced upper town there are splendid views to be enjoyed over the lower town across the river.

The Anglin and Creuse river valleys are particularly attractive, this being an area rich in curiously-shaped rocky outcrops and caves, picturesque villages, often clustered around a Romanesque church, and manor houses. The Benedictine

Hotels
Hôtel Domaine de l'Etape ★★
route de Belabre
☎ 54.37.18.02
Hôtel de Ile d'Avant ★★
route de Châteauroux
☎ 54.37.01.56
(and restaurant)
Hôtel du Théâtre ★★
☎ 54.37.68.69

Restaurants
Le Gambetta ★
☎ 54.37.02.03
Suisse-Océan ★
route de Poitiers
☎ 54.37.10.19
Au Vieux Château ★
☎ 54.37.03.26

SHOOTING IN THE LOIRE

abbey church at **Fontgombault** and the tiny village of **Angles-sur-l'Anglin** are worth special detours, the latter offering a spectacular panorama. A prime fishing and game shooting area too, the solitude of the wild area of marsh and meres around **La Brenne** to the north-east has its own appeal.

Leisure
Fishing Category 2 fishing on the Creuse, Anglin, Gartempe and Benaize rivers; also on the Etangs de Brenne.
Riding Centre Equestre et Pony Club L'Epinau, Ruffec-le-Château ☎ 54.37.72.63. Trips in horse-drawn carriages available from l'Attelage pour Tous ☎ 54.37.43.94 (as below).
Watersports A popular area for canoeing, week-long trips for families or groups of four-eight people are offered on the Anglin, Creuse and Gartempe rivers. Details from M. Lemenager, l'Attelage pour Tous, Les Tailles, St-Aigny, 3 km north of Le Blanc ☎ 54.37.43.94

BLOIS
Map ref. 121 F5
Pop 50,000
Orléans 58 km
Tours 61 km
Châteauroux 96 km
Paris 182 km
🛈 3 avenue Jean-Laigret
☎ 54.74.06.49

A charming city of great artistic and historic interest, with five centuries of history and architectural styles embodied in the stone of the magnificent château. Visually, there is much to please, from the multi-arched Pont Jacques-Gabriel spanning the wide River Loire, lined on either side by elegant town houses, to the St-Louis cathedral and the attractive views from the formal gardens close by. Blois is an excellent base for visiting a number of châteaux. Only 16 km away, and on the opposite bank of the river, is the beautiful **Château de Chambord**, the largest château of the Loire valley and a masterpiece of Renaissance architecture. The forests which surround it have viewing points to enable visitors to

Hotels
Hôtel Horset la Vallière ★★★
26 avenue Manoury
☎ 54.74.19.00
(and restaurant)
Hôtel de Medicis ★★★
2 allée François 1er
☎ 54.43.94.04
(and restaurant)
Novotel ★★★
rue de l'Almandin
La Chaussée Saint-Victor
☎ 54.78.33.57
(and restaurant)
Hôtel Anne de Bretagne ★★
31 avenue du Dr. Jean Laigret
☎ 54.78.05.38
Hôtel Arcade ★★
rue Jean-Moulin
☎ 54.78.24.14
(and restaurant)
Hôtel Campanile ★★
rue de la Vallée-Maillard
☎ 54.74.44.66
(and restaurant)
Hôtel les Trois Marches ★★
58 rue Foulerie
☎ 54.74.48.86
(and restaurant)

Camping
Camping du Lac de Loire ★★★★
☎ 54.78.82.05
750 places, Apr-Oct

Youth Hostel
rue de l'Hôtel Pasquier
Les Grouëts
☎ 54.78.27.21
Mar-Nov

Restaurants
Brasserie St-Jacques ★★
rue Auguste Poulain
☎ 54.78.54.57

BLOIS AT NIGHT

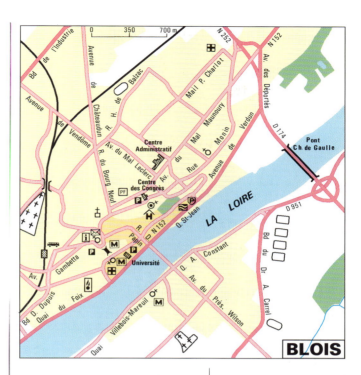

observe the deer and wild boar in their natural habitat.

Other châteaux in the area include the richly furnished, classically elegant **Cheverny** and **Chaumont**, while the small château at **Talcy**, north-east of Blois, and **Beauregard** to the south, should also be included in excursions. Most of these châteaux can be reached easily and pleasantly by bicycle and the Tourist Office can provide maps and itineraries for cyclists. A major sports complex has been created at the **Lac du Loire**, a short distance along the right bank, with extensive watersports facilities.

Leisure

Boat Trips Bookable through the Tourist Office and operating between Chaumont and Amboise, Apr-Oct.

Châteaux Château de Blois: open all year with son-et-lumière *Apr-Sep* ☎ 54.78.06.62. Château de Chambord: open all year ☎ 54.20.31.32 also stages son-et-lumière, *Jul-Oct*.

Cycling Cycles for hire from Cycles Leblond, 44 Levée des Tuileries ☎ 54.73.30.13 and from the SNCF station.

Fishing Category 2 fishing on the Loire.

Flights Bookable through the Tourist Office and operating from the Du Breuil aerodrome, light aircraft flights of anything from 25 mins to almost 2 hrs give unforgettable bird's eye views of the châteaux. Helicopter flights of between 10 mins and 1 hr, over the châteaux, operate from Blois-Hélistation, Pont Charles de Gaulle ☎ 54.74.35.52 min. four passengers.

Golf 18-hole course at Golf du Château de

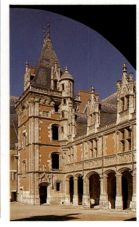

BLOIS CHATEAU

THE LOIRE

Cheverny, La Rousselière, 41700 Contres
☎ 54.79.24.70
Guided Tours Walking tours of the old part of the city depart from the château
☎ 54.74.16.06
Museum Natural history museum, rue Anne de Bretagne ☎ 54.74.13.89 housed in the 15th-century Couvent des Jacobins.
Riding Centre Equestre, Levée des Tuileries, La Chaussée-St-Victor
☎ 54.74.59.67
Walking In the Forêt de Blois.
Watersports Sailing, canoeing, water-skiing and pedalos at Lac de Loire, on the right bank in the direction of Orléans. Canoe hire and tuition available from Levée des Tuileries, La Chaussée-St-Victor ☎ 54.78.65.90

BOURGES
Map ref. 134 F1
Pop 80,000
Orléans 108 km
Blois 108 km
Tours 147 km
Paris 226 km
🄸 21 rue Victor-Hugo
☎ 48.24.75.33

In the very centre of France, this great cathedral city abounds in art and architectural treasures, with the picturesque buildings of medieval Bourges at its heart: the Palais Jacques Coeur built in 1443, the Renaissance Musée de l'Hôtel Lallemant, the 14th-century houses of the pedestrianized rue Bourbonnoux and the vast and majestic Gothic cathedral of St-Etienne. In April the festival Printemps de Bourges draws distinguished artists and thousands of visitors.

There are also several public gardens to enjoy such as the Jardin de l'Archevêché with its roses and lawns, and the Prés Fichaux beside the River Yèvre. Though the surrounding country is famous for its Charolais cattle and for its vast expanses of fields of rape seed, Berry today is essentially the same mysterious, nostalgically beautiful country of its novelist Alain-Fournier.

Leisure
Cycling Cycles for hire from the SNCF station.
Golf Windy, lakeside 9-hole course at Golf de Bourges, route de Lazenay, Val d'Auron ☎ 48.21.20.01

Hotels
Angleterre et Windsor ★★★
1 place des 4 Piliers
☎ 48.24.68.51
(and restaurant)
Hôtel Grand Argentier ★★
9 rue Parerie
☎ 48.70.84.31
(and restaurant)
Hôtel France ★★
place Henri Mirepied
☎ 48.70.31.12
(and restaurant)
Ibis ★★
rue V. Jankelevitch
☎ 48.65.89.99
(and restaurant)
Hôtel Olympia ★★
avenue d'Orléans
☎ 48.70.49.84

Camping
Municipal ★★★
boulevard de l'Industrie
☎ 48.20.16.85
116 places

Youth Hostel
22 rue Henri Sellier
☎ 48.24.58.09
open all year

Restaurants
Le Jacques Coeur ★★★★
3 place Jacques Coeur
☎ 48.70.12.72
Le Berry ★★★
place du Général Leclerc
☎ 48.24.48.40

OLD BOURGES

GAZETTEER 77

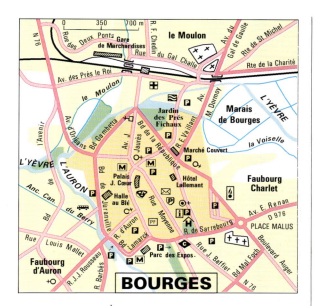

Guided Tours The Tourist Office organizes daily guided tours of old Bourges, both during the day and on Fri and Sat evenings.

Loisirs Accueil Cycling eight-day round trip, with accommodation and onward transportation of luggage arranged, past the historic monuments and along river and canal paths. Priced at 2,575FF, details of this and other trips from Loisirs Accueil Cher. Also half-day helicopter flights along the Route Jacques-Coeur leave from and return to Bourges, making two stops at monuments en route; min. five passengers. Details from Loisirs Accueil Cher (address on page 27).

Museums Several of interest: Musée du Berry, Hôtel Cujas, rue des Arènes, closed Tues and Sun morning; Musée des Arts Decoratifs, Hôtel Lallemant, rue Bourbonnaux, closed Mon and Sun morning; Musée Esteve, Hôtel des Echevins, rue Edouard Branly, closed Tues and Sun morning; and Musée de l'Ecole, rue de la Thaumassière, open Wed.

Watersports The large artificial lake, Lac du Val d'Auron, sees the sailing of yachts as well as model sailing boats.

ST-ETIENNE CATHEDRAL

BOURGUEIL
Map ref. 128 D1
Pop 5,000
Chinon 17 km
Tours 46 km
Blois 104 km
Orléans 161 km
Paris 270 km
🅱 la Mairie
☎ 47.97.70.50
July-Sep

A small town in vineyard country, it is indeed a wine-grower's village, with an elegant market place and its own wine museum, Cave Touristique de la Dive-bouteille, where wine tasting is featured. The climate here is ideal for the cultivation of the grape, so its famous vineyards dominate the Loire valley and there are plenty of opportunities to taste and buy the excellent local red wine.
For those on the château trail, those nearby include Langeais, Villandry, Ussé and Azay-le-Rideau. Fontevraud l'Abbaye, just acrosss the river, is the burial place of Henry II, Eleanor of Aquitaine, Richard the Lionheart and Isabelle of Angoulême, wife of King John.
Leisure
Golf See Chinon.
Wine Annual festival in Apr. Tastings and cellar tours at Cave Touristique de la Dive-bouteille ☎ 47.97.72.01, 2 km away in a cave near Chevrette.

Hotels
L'Ecu de France *
rue de Tours
☎ 47.97.70.18
(and restaurant)
Le Thouarsais *
place Hublin
☎ 47.97.72.05

Camping
La Grande Prairie **
☎ 47.97.85.62
88 places

Restaurant
Le Moulin Bleu
☎ 47.97.71.41

BRIARE
Map ref. 125 F4
Pop 6,000
Orléans 75 km
Blois 125 km
Paris 160 km
Tours 183 km
🅱 place de l'Eglise
☎ 38.31.24.51

An attractive small town whose principal claim to fame is a comparatively modern piece of architecture. Between 1890 and 1897, work was carried out to connect the Canal de Briare with the Canal Latéral to the Loire, by lifting the waterway across the dangerously unpredictable river. The engineer-designer of this remarkable work, a 664 m long canal-bridge, the famous *Ruban d'Eau* or 'Ribbon of Water', was Gustave Eiffel, who had just completed the construction of a certain tower in Paris. The narrow canal-bridge is still used today for commercial traffic, and as a cruising thoroughfare is the largest of its type in the world.
The busy marina here caters for the many barges and water-borne holidaymakers cruising to and from Burgundy country, with pedestrians able to watch their passage and appreciate the wonderful views from walkways the length of this extraordinary bridge.
Leisure
Boat Trips Leisurely cruises enjoying a meal as the countryside glides past.

Hotels
Hôtel Hostellerie le Canal **
19 quai Pont-Canal
☎ 38.31.22.54
(and restaurant)
Hôtel du Cerf **
22-24 boulevard Buyser
☎ 38.37.00.80
(and restaurant)

Camping
Le Martinet **
☎ 38.31.24.51
250 places

THE BRIDGE-CANAL AT BRIARE

Château Set amidst lake and parkland designed by le Nôtre, the Château la Bussière is not only richly furnished but, given the present owner's large fishing collection, is of particular interest to the specialist angler. Nicknamed the 'Château des Pêcheurs', it is located 12 km north of Briare. Open daily Mar-Nov, closed Tues.
Fishing Category 2 fishing on the Loire and canals.
Golf See Sully-sur-Loire.
Loisirs Accueil One-way or return cruising holidays on the canals of the Loiret or the Canal Latéral in boats equipped for four-twelve people or in bateaux-hôtels for extra luxury. Prices range according to season and details are available from Loisirs Accueil Cher (address on page 27).
Museum Situated in a disused lime kiln factory, the Musée de l'Automobile houses vintage cars, motorbikes and bicycles. Open daily ☎ 38.31.20.34

THE PLANTAGENETS

The Plantagenets, so called because they took as their family emblem the *genêt* or broom plant, were the powerful Counts of Anjou who, during the 12th century, challenged the supremacy of their feudal overlords, the Capetian kings of France.

When Henry Plantagenet succeeded his father in 1151, he already possessed Anjou, Touraine, Maine and Normandy. By a judicious marriage to Eleanor of Aquitaine, the divorced wife of Louis VII of France, he acquired considerably more territory, and three years later succeeded the childless King Stephen of England. As Henry II of England he ruled a vast empire which stretched from Hadrian's Wall to the Pyrenees.

Henry's ambition was only matched by his tireless energy. Although Chinon and Angers were the centres of his empire, Henry was constantly on the move. Had it not been for the rivalry of his three sons, Richard, Geoffrey and John, and the constant plotting of his indomitable wife, Eleanor, Henry might well have succeeded in taking the throne of France. On his death in 1189, his son Richard (the Lionheart) succeeded. Richard spent most of his reign on the Third Crusade and on his return in 1199 was mortally wounded at Chalus in the Limousin.

John then came to the Plantagenet throne but proved no match for the wily Philip Augustus of France. By 1205, John had lost all his French possessions to the French king, and was forever after known as John 'Lackland'. After John's death in 1216 the Plantagenets concentrated on their English possessions and it was not until the next century that their descendant, Edward III, revived the challenge to the king of France and initiated the Hundred Years War.

Henry II, Richard I and Eleanor are all buried in Fontevraud l'Abbaye, on the borders of Anjou and Poitou; their descendants lie in Westminster Abbey.

The Plantagenets

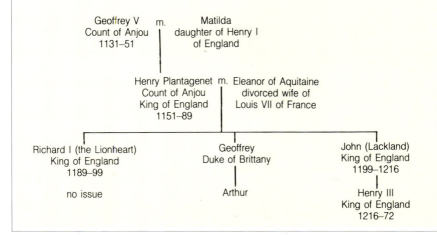

THE LOIRE

CHARTRES
Pop 40,000
Orléans 73 km
Paris 88 km
Blois 103 km
Tours 141 km
🛈 place de la Cathédrale
☎ 37.21.50.00

In addition to the pull of the magnificent cathedral, the twin spires of which are visible for miles across the flat agricultural land, Chartres attracts visitors for whom it can provide an excellent base for exploring the Ile-de-France region to the south of Paris, as well as the Loire valley itself.

There are many 16th-century houses gathered round the cathedral in the medieval upper town, and in the lower town hump-backed bridges linking riverside walks to the Pont de la Courtille where small rowing boats can be hired. Just to the north in the Eure valley is the **Château de Maintenon** with gardens by Le Nôtre, an aqueduct constructed by Vauban and an exceptional golf course in the grounds. This is a delightful area for discovery by balloon, canoe, horseback or bicycle or at the leisurely pace of a gypsy caravan.

Hotels
Hôtel le Grand Monarque ***
22 place des Epars
☎ 37.21.00.72
(and **** restaurant)
Hôtel Mercure Chatelet ***
avenue Jehan-de-Beauce
☎ 37.21.78.00
(and restaurant)
Hôtel Novotel ***
avenue Marcel Proust
☎ 37.34.80.30
(and restaurant)

Camping
Municipal Les Bords de l'Eure ***
☎ 37.28.79.43
105 places

Youth Hostel
23 avenue Neigre
☎ 37.34.27.64

Restaurants
Le Grand Monarque ****
22 place des Epars
☎ 37.21.00.72
Henri IV ****
rue du Soleil-d'Or
☎ 37.36.01.55
La Vieille Maison ****
rue au Lait
☎ 37.34.10.67
Le Buisson Ardent ***
rue au Lait
☎ 37.34.04.66
Le Minou **
rue de Lattre-de-Tassigny
☎ 37.21.10.68

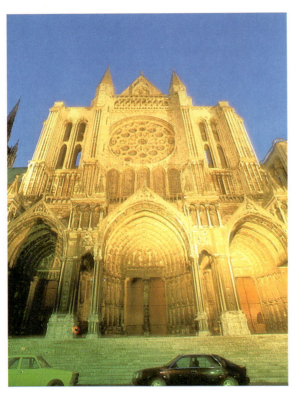

CHARTRES CATHEDRAL AT NIGHT

Leisure
Art Sited in the old episcopal palace, the Musée des Beaux Arts, 29 cloître Notre Dame ☎ 37.36.41.39 houses a permanent collection of paintings, tapestries, enamels and sculpture, closed Tues. Modern art from this century is represented at La Maison Picassiette, rue de Repos ☎ 37.36.41.39, open Easter-Sep. Close to the cathedral in rue du Cardinal Pie is the Centre International du Vitrail (stained glass), open daily throughout the year, closed Mon.

Ballooning Both operators based near Maintenon, flights are available through Montgolfière Pégase Evasion, 4 rue Normande, Epernon ☎ 37.83.44.16 and Montgolfière Club Aérostatique d'Ile de France ☎ 37.27.60.05
Château Château de Maintenon open daily, Apr-Oct ☎ 37.23.00.09
Cycling Cycles for hire from the SNCF station.
Golf 18-hole course just to the north at Golf du Château de Maintenon, 28130 Maintenon ☎ 37.27.18.09; also 18-hole private course at Golf du Perche, Nogent-le-Rotrou, Vallée des Aulnes, 28400 Souancé-au-Perche ☎ 37.52.10.33
Guided Tours Daily guided walking tours plus audio taped tours of the old part of the city are available for hire, and a small tourist train leaves regularly from the Tourist Office.
Loisirs Accueil The following holiday options are all bookable through Loisirs Accueil Eure-et-Loir (address on page 27). Hot-air balloon flights over the Château de Maintenon cost 1,350FF or 510FF by ultralight. Canoeing and kayaking courses in the Eure, Huisne, Loir and Conie valleys, including accommodation under canvas or in a hotel cost 2,300FF. Fishing weeks at Thiron Gardais with bungalow accommodation cost 850FF between Apr-Sep; or week or weekend trips in a four-berth gypsy caravan in the Eure valley are priced at 1,300FF; a day spent on two- or four-horse carriage tours of the Perche country costs 500FF.
Riding Pony-Club du Pays Chartrain, route de Nogent-le-Phaye ☎ 37.30.10.10

CHARTRES CATHEDRAL

CHATEAUDUN
Map ref. 121 A5
Pop 16,000
Chartres 44 km
Orléans 49 km
Blois 58 km
Tours 97 km
Paris 131 km
🛈 1 rue de Luynes
☎ 37.45.22.46

In a pretty setting on the River Loir, its tall château rising from a rocky outcrop, the austere fortress of seemingly massive strength looks down on the meandering and languid course of the river. This is a rich agricultural region south of Chartres, Châteaudun, with its small squares and overhanging 16th-century houses being the chief market town for the area. A tree-shaded avenue above the Loir gives views reaching to the Perche hillsides.

Leisure
Château A combination of medieval, Gothic and Renaissance, the château once belonged to Jehan de Dunois, companion-in-arms to Joan of Arc. Open throughout the year ☎ 37.45.22.70, it offers a son-et-lumière production entitled Châteaudun et ses incendies or 'Châteaudun and its fires'.
Cycling Cycles for hire from the SNCF station.
Fishing Category 1 and 2 fishing on the Loir and its tributaries.
Loisirs Accueil Fly fishing along a special stretch of water, together with full board, fishing rights and packed lunches, can be booked through Loisirs Accueil Eure-et-Loir (address on page 27).
Museum Boasting an outstanding natural history collection on birds and an important

Hotels
Hôtel Armorial ★★
59 rue Gambetta
☎ 37.45.19.57
Hôtel de Beauce ★★
50 rue de Jallans
☎ 37.45.14.75
Hôtel de la Rose ★★
12 rue Lambert-Licors
☎ 37.45.21.83
(and ★★★★ restaurant)

Camping
Municipal du Moulin à Tan ★★
☎ 37.45.05.34
133 places

Restaurants
L'Arnaudière ★★
rue Saint-Lubin
☎ 37.45.98.98
La Licorne ★★
6 place du 18 octobre
☎ 37.45.32.32
Aux Trois Pastoraux ★★
rue André Gillet
☎ 37.45.74.40

THE LOIRE

Egyptology section is the Musée des Beaux Arts et d'Histoire Naturelle, rue Toufaire ☎ 37.45.55.36
Riding Centre Equestre Nessus Club, clos de Comblais, route de St-Denis les Ponts ☎ 37.45.25.25
Walking The Tourist Office can provide local short-distance itineraries, with the Grottes du Foulon, river-formed caves, of particular interest.

CHATEAUNEUF-SUR-LOIRE
Map ref. 123 C6
Pop 6,000
Orléans 26 km
Blois 83 km
Paris 132 km
Tours 143 km
🛈 place Aristide Briand
☎ 38.58.44.79

The shady banks of the wide and languid River Loire provide a fishing paradise for anglers, while the museum here recalls days when the river was busy with traffic. The town is neat and quite modern in parts, and leisurely walks amongst the ancient plane trees or the gorgeous rhododendrons (flowering in May), azaleas and orange trees in the château's park garden, are a delight.
Close by at 3 km is the church of **Germigny-des-Prés** with its exquisite 9th-century mosaic of several thousand pieces, and the impressive 12th-century abbey of **St-Benoît** at 9 km, whose fine Romanesque basilica is visible for some distance and in which services continue to be sung in Gregorian chant.
Leisure
Fishing Category 2 fishing on the Loire.
Golf 18-hole private course at Golf du Val de Loire-Orléans, Château de la Touche, Donnery, 45450 Fay-aux-Loges ☎ 38.59.25.15; see also Beaugency, Montargis and Sully-sur-Loire.
Museum Situated within the château, the Musée de la Marine de Loire is open weekends, Jun-Oct.

Hotels
Hôtel Hostellerie du Parc (La Capitainerie) **
Grande-Rue
☎ 38.58.42.16
(and *** restaurant)
Nouvel Hôtel du Loiret **
4 place Aristide-Briand
☎ 38.58.42.28
(and restaurant)
Hôtel Auberge du Point du Jour *
44 avenue Albert-Viger
☎ 38.58.95.52

Camping
La Maltournée **
☎ 38.58.42.46
200 places

CHATEAUNEUF CHATEAU

CHAUMONT-SUR-LOIRE
Map ref. 130 B3
Pop 1,000
Amboise 18 km
Blois 19 km
Tours 43 km
Orléans 77 km
Paris 201 km
🛈 la Mairie
☎ 54.20.98.41

'Hell hath no fury like a woman scorned.' This is the rather austere fortress for which Catherine de Médicis forced her husband Henry II's mistress Diane de Poitiers to relinquish Chenonceau. She was not to stay here long.
The terrace overlooking the river offers splendid views and the grounds contain ancient trees. The 19th-century stables are extraordinary in their luxury, some being lined in velvet. These date from the period when the château was owned by the de Broglie family, wealthy and flamboyant and given to such extravagance.

Leisure
Château Château, grounds and stables open daily, throughout the year
☎ 54.20.98.03
Wine Tastings and cellar tours at Caves Brossillon, Domaine de Lusqueneau, Mesland ☎ 54.70.28.23 and Château Gaillard, route d'Onzain, Mesland
☎ 54.70.27.14

Hotel
Hôtel Hostellerie du Château ★★★
rue du Maréchal-de-Lattre-de-Tassigny
☎ 54.90.98.04
(and restaurant)

Camping
Camping Grosse Grève ★★
☎ 54.20.93.95
180 places

CHINON

CHINON
Map ref. 128 E2
Pop 9,000
Saumur 31 km
Tours 47 km
Blois 107 km
Orléans 164 km
Paris 275 km
🛈 12 rue Voltaire
☎ 47.93.17.85

This lovely old town stretches along the tree-lined banks of the Vienne, its turreted dwellings dominated by the enormous ruined defensive works high on the escarpment above. Built between the 10th and 15th centuries, the château is closely linked with figures from the history books, Richard the Lionheart, Joan of Arc and Césare Borgia.
An area of great beauty, with vineyards, oak and fir-tree forests, numerous excursions are possible, and this is a particularly good region to discover by bicycle. A medieval market is held on the first weekend in August and elegant Azay-le-Rideau, on the banks of the Indre, is close by, as is La Devinière, the childhood home of Rabelais, son of a Chinon lawyer.

Leisure
Château Open daily ☎ 47.93.13.45, closed Dec-Jan.
Cycling Cycles for hire from the SNCF station.
Fishing Category 2 fishing on the Vienne.

Hotels
Château de Marcay ★★★★
Marcay, 7 km south
☎ 47.93.03.47
(and restaurant)
Château de Danzay ★★★★
Baumont-en-Véron
5 km Chinon
☎ 47.58.46.86
Hôtel Chéops ★★★
Centre St-Jacques
☎ 47.98.46.46
(and restaurant)
Le Chris'Hôtel ★★
12 place Jeanne-d'Arc
☎ 47.93.36.92
Grand Hôtel de la Boule d'Or ★★
quai Jeanne-d'Arc
☎ 47.93.03.13
(and restaurant)
Hostellerie Gargantua ★★
rue Voltaire
☎ 47.93.04.71
(and restaurant)

Golf Attractive 18-hole woodland public course at Golf de Saint-Hilaire, Centre des Loisirs Loudun-Roiffé, 86120 Les Trois Moutiers ☎ 49.98.78.06
Guided Tours Audio tapes can be hired from the Tourist Office for walking tours.
Nuclear Power Station Guided visits to the installation are possible by prior booking. Contact Site Electronucléaire de Chinon et Centre d'informations Nucléaires, BP 80, 37420 Avoine ☎ 47.98.90.79. Foreign visitors must present their passports in order to gain entry.
Riding Carriage trips available from Centre d'Attelage du Grand-Palefroi, St-Lazaire ☎ 47.93.30.75
Steam Train Short trips on a 1920s steam train between Chinon, Champigny-sur-Veude and Richelieu through the Touraine countryside; weekends only, May-Sep. Enquire at the Tourist Office.
Watersports Canoe hire and tuition available from 25 rue du Faubourg St-Jacques ☎ 47.93.39.59
Wine Tastings and cellar tours at Cave Montplaisir, quai Pasteur ☎ 47.93.20.75

Camping
Municipal Ile Auger **
☎ 47.93.08.35
150 places

Youth Hostel
rue Descartes
☎ 47.93.10.48

GIEN
Map ref. 125 E4
Pop 10,000
Orléans 65 km
Blois 116 km
Paris 158 km
Tours 174 km
🛈 rue Anne-de-Beaujeu
☎ 38.67.25.28

Fine views across rooftops and along the Loire extend from the terraces of the brick château built at the end of the 15th century for Anne-de-Beaujeu, daughter of Louis XI. Today the building houses a specialist hunting museum, the many paintings and exhibits covering all aspects of the sport. The town itself, carefully restored after bomb damage suffered during the last war, has long been involved in producing *faïencerie*, decorative pottery.
A little distance to the north towards Montargis, is the **Les Barres** arboretum which, with over 10,000 trees and botanical species cultivated from all over the world, is one of the most impressive in Europe.

Leisure
Arboretum Situated midway between Gien and Montargis, 21 km north at Nogent-sur-Vernisson. Open daily, afternoons only at weekends, Mar-Nov ☎ 38.97.60.20
Cycling Cycles for hire from the SNCF station.
Fishing Category 2 fishing of the River Loire with numerous small lakes and ponds in the Forêt d'Orléans and the Sologne.
Golf See Montargis and Sully-sur-Loire.
Loisirs Accueil Six-day cycling and gourmand tour combined. Round trip leaving from Sury-aux-Bois through wooded countryside, Mar-Nov. Price 3,100FF per person includes accommodation in ** or *** hotels, hire of cycle, detailed itinerary and onward transport of luggage. Contact Loisirs Accueil Loiret (address on page 27).
Museum Musée International de la Chasse is housed within the château.
Nuclear Power Station Midway between Gien and Sully-sur-Loire, information

Hotels
Hôtel du Rivage ***
1 quai de Nice
☎ 38.67.20.53
(and restaurant)
Hôtel Beau Site **
13 quai de Nice
☎ 38.67.36.05
(and restaurant)
Hôtel Sanotel **
21 quai de Sully
☎ 38.67.61.46

Camping
Municipal **
quai de Sully
☎ 38.67.12.50
400 places

Restaurant
La Loire *
18 quai Lenoir
☎ 38.67.00.75

GAZETTEER

LES BARRES ARBORETUM

**LE GRAND-
PRESSIGNY**
Map ref. 137 B5
Pop 1,000
Tours 57 km
Blois 99 km
Orléans 155 km
Paris 280 km
🅘 Café le Borne
Grande-Rue
☎ 47.94.91.36

centre open daily. Group and individual visits to the installation proper by prior written appointment only and at least two weeks in advance. Contact Centre de Production Nucléaire de Dampierre-en-Burly, Relations Publiques, BP 18, 45570 Ouzouer-sur-Loire ☎ 38.29.70.04. Foreign visitors must present their passports.
Watersports Water-skiing, canoeing, rowing and sailing on the Etang de Puits, 25 km south-west.

High above this small rural village in the pretty Claise river valley stand portions of a 12th-century feudal château. Today this houses a museum of prehistory with a large concentration of flint finds, a collection which is amongst the best in the world. Otherwise this is a place for walking, riding and peaceful riverside pursuits.
The birthplace of the great French philosopher René Descartes, together with a museum devoted to his memory, is nearby in the small town renamed in his honour. The major châteaux of the Loire are within easy range, but one which might otherwise escape attention is the 15th-century fortress **Château de la Guerche**, 8 km west.
Leisure
Fishing Category 1 fishing on the Aigronne and category 2 fishing on the Claise.
Golf See La Roche-Posay.

Camping
Camping de la Croix Marron **
☎ 47.94.90.37
33 places

ISSOUDUN
Map ref. 140 B2
Pop 15,000
Bourges 37 km
Blois 101 km
Orléans 115 km
Tours 127 km
Paris 240 km
🛈 place St-Cyr
☎ 54.21.74.57

Amidst the rich, flat agricultural region of Berry, Issoudun hosts a large Saturday market and several fairs throughout the year. Synonymous with straightforward cuisine, for the most part based on pork, mutton and poultry dishes, Balzac remarked of this area: 'On ne dîne pas aussi luxueusement en Berry qu'à Paris, mais on y dîne mieux' – 'You may not dine as luxuriously in Berry as you do in Paris, but you will eat better'.

The 12th-century white cylindrical keep, the Tour Blanche, was constructed by Richard the Lionheart, the ramparts beneath it commanding extensive views. The town is, in part, situated on the side of a hill, the valley at the foot of which is fed by the River Théols.

Leisure
Museum Musée Saint-Roch is housed in the 15th-century hospice and has an impressively re-created pharmacy of the 16th and 17th centuries, closed Tues.
Riding Les Ecuries de la Ferté, Château de la Ferté at Reuilly, 14 km from Issoudun ☎ 48.51.75.87 offer woodland rides or day or longer treks. Ranch R at Mareuil-sur-Arnon, just south, offers American 'Wild-West' style outings ☎ 48.69.92.51

Hotels
Hôtel de la Cognette ✱✱✱
rue des Minimes
☎ 54.21.21.83
Hôtel de France et du Commerce ✱✱✱
3 rue Pierre-Brossolette
☎ 54.21.00.65

Camping
Municipal les Taupeaux ✱✱
route de Vierzon
☎ 54.03.13.46
50 places

Restaurants
La Cognette ✱✱✱✱
boulevard Stalingrad
☎ 54.21.21.83
Les Trois Rois ✱✱
rue Pierre-Brossolette
☎ 54.21.00.65

SON-ET-LUMIERE
Several châteaux put on night-time *son-et-lumière* productions during the summer which are both educational and great fun.

Amboise (Indre-et-Loire)
Entitled *A la cour du Roy François*, this is a lively re-creation of Renaissance courtly life with 400 participants in period costume.
Dates: every few days Jun-Aug, and early Sep.
Duration: 1 hr 40 mins; starts 10.30pm.
Price: 60FF for adults, 35-45FF for children.
Bookable through: Tourist Office ☎ 47.57.09.28 or Association Renaissance d'Amboise ☎ 47.57.14.47.

Azay-le-Rideau (Indre-et-Loire)
Entitled *Puisque de vous nous n'avons autre visage,* this spectacle takes place in the grounds of the château with costumed actors.
Dates: every evening 24 May-23 Sep.
Duration: 1 hr; starts 10.30pm.
Price: 40FF.
Bookable through: Direction Départementale du Tourisme, 9 rue de Buffon, Tours ☎ 47.31.48.05.

Blois (Loir-et-Cher)
In the château courtyard itself, this spectacle is entitled *Les Esprits Aiment la Nuit.*
Dates: every evening from 15 Jun-29 Sep.
Duration: 40 mins.; starts 10.30pm.
Price: 23FF for adults, 17FF for children.
Bookable through: Tourist Office ☎ 54.74.06.49.

Chambord (Loir-et-Cher)
Along the theme of *Une journée de François 1er,* or a day in the life of François I.
Dates: nightly from Jul-Oct.
Bookable through: Château de Chambord ☎ 54.20.31.50.

Chenonceau (Indre-et-Loire)
Entitled *Au temps des Dames de Chenonceau,* this takes place in the château grounds.
Dates: mid Jun-9 Sep.
Duration: 45 mins; starts 10.15pm.
Price: 30FF for adults, 20FF for children.
Bookable through: Château de Chenonceau ☎ 47.23.90.07.

ISSOUDUN

Cheverny (Loir-et-Cher)
Entitled *Spectacle Louis XII*, this production plays out the history of the château.
Dates: regularly in Jul and Aug.
Duration: 1 hr 20 mins; starts 10.30pm.
Price: 70FF.
Bookable through: Blois Tourist Office ☎ 54.74.06.49.

Loches (Indre-et-Loire)
Entitled *Jeanne d'Arc ou la force du Lys*, this production leads through the medieval heart of the town.
Dates: regularly in Jul and Aug; starts 10pm.
Duration: 1 hr 30 mins.
Price: 50FF for adults, 30FF for children.
Bookable through: Tourist Office ☎ 47.59.07.98.

Saché (Indre-et-Loire)
Entitled *Balzac et la Vallée du Lys*, it recalls the life of the writer and is staged in the château grounds.
Dates: late Jun and regularly in Jul; starts 10.30pm.
Duration: 1 hr 25 mins.
Price: 45FF for adults, 30FF for children.
Bookable through: la Mairie, Saché ☎ 47.26.86.65.

Valençay (Indre)
Entitled *La belle captive*, it tells the love story of André Chenier and Aimée de Coigny and is staged in the beautiful château grounds.
Dates: regularly in Aug; starts 10pm.
Duration: 1 hr 50 mins.
Price: 60FF for adults, 30FF for children.
Bookable through: Capval, Valençay ☎ 54.00.14.33 and ☎ 54.00.04.42 in season.

Vendôme (Loir-et-Cher)
Entitled *Vendôme, la folie-dieu*, it tells of the lives of Jeanne d'Albret and Antoine de Bourbon, Duke and Duchess of Vendôme, and is staged in the château grounds.
Dates: regularly in Jul and Aug; starts 10.30pm.
Duration: 1 hr 30 mins.
Price: 80FF for adults, 50FF for children.
Bookable through: Association 'Les Compagnons du Lion d'Azur', avenue Gérard-Yvon, Vendôme ☎ 54.77.10.60.

LANGEAIS
Map ref. 128 D3
Pop 4,000
Tours 26 km
Chinon 29 km
Blois 84 km
Orléans 141 km
Paris 250 km
🛈 la Mairie
☎ 47.96.58.22

The celebrated Château de Langeais, where Charles VIII married the fifteen year-old Duchess Anne of Brittany in 1491, has all the external appearances of a medieval fortified stronghold. The interior, however, with its rich decor and furnishings, has a much more domestic feel with waxwork figures re-creating the wedding scene at the exact spot where the couple stood five centuries ago. From a lovely enclosed courtyard the formal gardens rise to the base of a ruined 10th-century keep, believed to be the oldest in France, and built by Foulques Nerra, Count of Anjou. The town itself runs below the château and along the right bank of the Loire and is best viewed from the opposite side.
By crossing the river at this point, thus avoiding Tours, visits can be made to the cluster of châteaux nearby – those of Villandry, Azay-le-Rideau, Ussé and Chinon.

Leisure
Château Open daily, Mar-Nov; closed Tues, Nov-Mar ☎ 47.96.72.60
Cycling Cycles for hire from the SNCF station.
Fishing Category 2 fishing on the Loire and Roumer rivers.
Golf See Tours.

Hotels
Hôtel Hosten ***
rue Gambetta
☎ 47.96.82.12
(and ****restaurant)
La Duchesse Anne **
10 rue de Tours
☎ 47.96.82.03
(and restaurant)

Camping
Municipal **
☎ 47.96.85.80
66 places

LANGEAIS CHATEAU

LOCHES
Map ref. 130 F2
Pop 7,000
Tours 41 km
Blois 66 km
Orléans 123 km
Paris 247 km
🛈 place de la Marne
☎ 47.59.07.98

Amidst pretty countryside this is a pleasant medieval town on the Indre, of great architectural and historic interest. The neat white faces of the old houses of the upper town contrast with the sinister fortifications of the massive *Donjon* whose grisly dungeons and dank cells buried deep within it occupy several floors below ground.
The royal Château de Loches, at the other end of the medieval part of town, has a gentler aspect. The 13th-century tower of the château is named 'the Beautiful Agnès Tower' after Agnès Sorel, the mistress of Charles VII, who lived here until her suspiciously early death. She was, incidentally, the first 'official' mistress of a king of France, and there is a fine marble tomb to her memory.

Hotels
Hôtel George Sand **
rue Quintefol
☎ 47.59.39.74
(and restaurant)
Grand Hôtel de France **
rue Picois
☎ 47.59.00.32
(and restaurant)
Hôtel la Tour St-Antoine **
place de la Marne
☎ 47.59.01.06
(and restaurant)

Camping
Municipal *
rue Quintefol
☎ 47.59.05.91
75 places

LOCHES CHATEAU

In the Great Hall, Joan of Arc met and persuaded Charles to go to Reims to be crowned, and in the Vieux Logis a copy of the proceedings of her subsequent trial is displayed. From the terrace above there is a superb view over the small town and along the river valley.

There are motoring routes following the course of the pretty River Indre and further places of interest to be sought out along the attractive Indrois river valley, this area of the Touraine both inviting and rewarding casual exploration.

Leisure

Château Open daily, 15 Mar-30 Sep; closed Wed, 1 Oct-14 Mar ☎ 47.59.01.32 with *son-et-lumière* productions all summer.

Cycling Cycles for hire from the SNCF station.

Fishing Category 2 fishing on the Indre.

Guided Tours Walking tours of the old town are available from the Tourist Office.

Loisirs Accueil 40 km a day, nine-day cycling circuit of the Touraine, Chinonais, Val de Vienne and Val d'Indre countryside. Cycle hire, bed and breakfast accommodation for eight nights, but no onward transport of luggage, is priced at 3,000FF per person. This and shorter trips bookable through Loisirs Accueil Indre-et-Loire (address on page 27).

Restaurant
La Gerbe d'Or
rue Balzac
☎ 47.59.06.38

AGNES SOREL (1422-50)

Born at La Brenne in the Touraine, Agnès Sorel was the daughter of a minor French noble. Her great beauty won her the position of Maid of Honour to the queen and not long after entering the royal household Charles VII took her to his bed.

As the king's mistress she became extremely powerful, her beauty being surpassed only by her intelligence. The rather weak king, used to the flattery of the Court, made a series of appointments of able subordinates, the choice of whom is largely attributed to the influence of his level-headed and well-informed mistress. These advisers helped the crown drive the remaining English from Normandy.

Agnès bore Charles four daughters and her beauty is preserved for posterity in the pious but profane bare-breasted portrait of *Virgin and Child* by the 15th-century artist Jean Fouquet. On her death from poisoning the finger of suspicion was pointed at **Jacques Coeur** who was forced to flee the country. There is a remarkable alabaster and marble effigy to Agnès Sorel's memory in the Château de Loches.

LORRIS
Map ref. 124 C3
Pop 3,000
Orléans 51 km
Blois 109 km
Paris 132 km
Tours 169 km
🅱 rue Gambetta
☎ 38.92.42.76

A peaceful little town on the edge of the forest of Orléans. This is, above all else, a walking and rich fishing area where large family groups, having come from Paris or Orléans for the weekend, will frequently be found enjoying the leafy walkways or the lakeside bathing area of the Lac du Bois.

Leisure
Fishing Category 2 fishing on the Canal d'Orléans and in numerous small lakes.
Golf See Châteauneuf-sur-Loire, Montargis and Sully-sur-Loire.
Watersports Sailing and windsurfing on the Lac du Bois, 5 km south-west.

Hotel
Hôtel le Sauvage **
place du Martroi
☎ 38.92.43.79
(and restaurant)

Camping
Plage et Forêt ***
☎ 38.92.32.00
150 places

MEHUN-SUR-YEVRE CHATEAU

MEHUN-SUR-YEVRE
Map ref. 133 E5
Pop 7,000
Bourges 17 km
Blois 91 km
Orléans 94 km
Tours 131 km
Paris 218 km
🅱 place du 14 juillet
☎ 48.57.35.51

Just north of Bourges and on the banks of the Cher, it was here that the dukes of Berry, with châteaux all over the country, had their favourite residence. The château built here by Jean de Berry, incomparably wealthy and a great acquirer of beautiful things, became the treasure-house for all his choicest possessions. Those familiar with the Duc de Berry's gorgeously illuminated prayer book, the *Très Riches Heures* or Book of Hours, a medieval calendar of courtly life in miniature, will see the château depicted in all its medieval splendour, rising from the waters of the Yèvre. Little remains of it today, however, bar two towers, one of which is now a ceramics museum.
There is a strong crafts tradition in the area, with stoneware pottery and porcelain the principal industries since the last century. At the foot of the ruins of the château, and entirely surrounded by water, the huge watermills which at one time supplied all the flour needs of the local bakers have been converted to house studios for over 200 craftsmen and artists. On exhibition here are the works of glass-blowers, engravers, stained glass and jewellery-makers, painters and sculptors and, of course, potters.
The little town was prominent in the life of

Hotels
Hôtel la Croix Blanche *
164 rue Jeanne d'Arc
☎ 48.57.30.01
(and restaurant)
Hôtel à l'Espérance *
15 place du 14 juillet
☎ 48.57.30.85
(and restaurant)
Hôtel le Lion d'Or *
place du 14 juillet
☎ 48.57.30.60
(and restaurant)

Camping
Municipal du Champ de Foire **
☎ 48.57.33.08
35 places

Restaurant
Les Abies
86 avenue Jean Chatelet
☎ 48.57.39.31

CAVE DWELLINGS

TROGLODYTES' CAVE DWELLINGS
Over the years, domestic architecture has used the soft, white limestone, tufa, dug from the riverbeds. Today, as in the past, it is used to make the cool, cave-like shelters for the local wines, as well as for the growing of mushrooms and for the building of homes for the people. Houses fronting the cliffs can be seen at Amboise, their rooms carved deep within the stone. Some of the best examples of 'troglodyte' dwellings are close to Montoire-sur-le-Loir at Les Roches-l'Evêque and Trôo, where the houses are linked by alleys and underground passages.

Charles VII and the politics of France, for it was here that he was proclaimed king in 1422, met with Joan of Arc in 1429 and 1430, and died in 1461.
Leisure
Crafts Open Wed-Sun, May-Sep; Thurs-Sun, Oct-Dec, Mar-Apr; the Centre Régional des Métiers d'Art, Les Grands Moulins ☎ 48.57.36.84
Fishing Category 2 fishing on the River Yèvre and Canal du Berry.

MENNETOU-SUR-CHER
Map ref. 132 D2
Pop 1,000
Romorantin-Lanthenay 15 km
Blois 58 km
Orléans 77 km
Tours 98 km
Paris 202 km
🅸 la Mairie
☎ 54.98.01.19

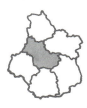

Along the banks of the Cher, this little fortified village presents its original medieval face, with ramparts, towers and gates still intact, and ancient houses lining the steep and winding streets. The Canal du Berry also runs past, adding to the pleasant watery nature of the place all of which invites leisurely exploration. The local speciality is *andouillettes*, small sausages made of chitterlings, and a fair to celebrate them is held in May.
Leisure
Fishing Category 2 fishing in the Cher and Canal du Berry.
Golf See Romorantin-Lanthenay.
Loisirs Accueil Enjoy leisurely travel through the Sologne and Cher valley by horse-drawn caravan. Equipped for four or five people, the price throughout the year is 3,000FF for a week, 1,200FF for a weekend. Departs from a base here or at several other locations, horse feed and a detailed itinerary supplied. Details from Loisirs Accueil Loir-et-Cher (address on page 27).

Hotel
Hôtel Lion d'Or **
rue Marcel Bailly
☎ 54.98.01.13
(and restaurant)

Camping
Camping Val Rose **
☎ 54.98.08.68
60 places

MONTARGIS

Map ref. 125 B4
Pop 18,000
Orléans 72 km
Paris 118 km
Blois 129 km
Tours 189 km
🛈 place du Pâtis
☎ 38.98.00.87

A popular and attractive town of elegant pale stone buildings on the River Loing with the Canal de Briare running parallel to it. Nicknamed 'the Venice of the Gâtinais', it boasts a total of 126 bridges and footbridges which criss-cross the waterways.

A Sunday tourist train service operates between June and September, travelling into Burgundy between Montargis and St-Sauveur and enabling visitors to appreciate at leisure the lovely Puisaye countryside of châteaux, pools, woods, canals, locks and cider-apple orchards.

Hotels
Hôtel Auberge de la Tour d'Auvergne **
20 rue Jean Jaurès
☎ 38.85.01.16
(and restaurant)
Hôtel la Gloire **
avenue du Général-de-Gaulle
☎ 38.85.04.69
(and ***restaurant)
Le Grand Hôtel de France *
44 place de la République
☎ 38.98.01.18

THE BRIARE CANAL, MONTARGIS

Leisure
Art French and foreign schools are well represented in the Musée Girodet in rue de la Chaussée, named after this local artist. Open all year, except Mon and Tues.
Cycling Cycles for hire from the SNCF station.
Fishing Category 2 fishing on the Briare and Orléans canals and on the Loing river.
Golf 18-hole private course at Golf de Vaugouard, chemin des Bois, Fontenay-sur-Loing, 45210 Ferrières-en-Gâtinais
☎ 38.95.81.52

Camping
Municipal de la Forêt ***
route de Paucourt
☎ 38.98.00.20
100 places

Youth Hostel
25 quai de la Port
Cepoy, 6 km from Montargis
☎ 38.93.25.45

MONTOIRE-SUR-LE-LOIR

Map ref. 120 E2
Pop 4,000
Vendôme 20 km
Blois 44 km
Tours 49 km
Orléans 93 km
Paris 191 km
🛈 la Mairie
☎ 54.85.00.29

Described as 'the prince of poets and the poet of princes', Pierre de Ronsard grew up in this valley. Born nearby in **Couture-sur-Loir** at the Manoir de la Poissonnière in 1524 the son of a courtier, he spent his early years as a page in royal service, later to become the centre of a small group of poets known as La Pléiade or the Pleiades, and then court poet to Henry II, Francis II and Charles IX successively. Founded in the 12th century for pilgrims following the Santiago de Compostela route, the delightful St-Gilles chapel possesses a unique fresco. An elegant town in an attractive part of the Loir valley amidst the Coteaux du Vendômois vineyards, a wine festival is held here on Whit Sunday and tastings are possible throughout the summer. The town also hosts a summer World Folk Festival in mid-August which attracts visitors and

Hotels
Hôtel du Cheval Rouge **
place Foch
☎ 54.85.07.05
(and **** restaurant)
Hôtel des Deux Châteaux *
avenue des Reclusages
☎ 54.85.01.99
(and restaurant)
Hôtel la Gerbe d'Or *
41 place Clémenceau
☎ 54.85.01.31

Camping
Municipal des Reclusages **
☎ 54.85.02.53
120 places

RONSARD

performers from all over the world, staging a colourful week-long celebration of dance and song.
Not to be missed is the little village of **Lavardin** 2 km south, which has been called 'the most French of all the villages of France' and is simply exquisite. Some of the best examples of 'troglodyte' dwellings are close by too; at **Les Roches-l'Evêque** 4 km east, and **Trôo** 6 km west, where the houses are linked by alleys and underground passages.

Leisure
Cycling Cycles for hire from M. Capponi, place Maréchal Foch ☎ 54.85.35.48 and from the campsite.
Fishing Category 1 and 2 fishing on the Loir.
Golf See Blois.
Guided Tours Tours of troglodyte villages for groups only; enquire at the Tourist Office.
Watersports Lac de Ronsard in Couture-sur-Loir offers water-skiing and microlight flying instruction ☎ 54.72.48.73

MONTRESOR
Map ref. 130 E3
Pop 500
Loches 18 km
Tours 55 km
Blois 62 km
Orléans 118 km
Paris 242 km
🛈 la Mairie
☎ 47.92.60.19

A sleepy village on the River Indrois, a tiny tributary of the Indre, with a name evocative of the riches inherited from its past. Well off the beaten track for the major Loire châteaux, this is a peaceful backwater in an attractive, tree-filled landscape.
Remains of a powerful fortress stronghold, once again the work of Foulques Nerra, form the basis for the elegant Renaissance château, whose twin towers and steeply gabled roof and the surrounding old houses are reflected in the still waters below. It was restored in the 19th century by the Polish Count Branicki, whose collection of paintings, furniture and mementoes of Polish royalty fill the rooms. There is also a particularly fine village church.
From here, an outing to **Valençay** to the east makes an interesting excursion. The 16th-century château, which has *son-et-*

Camping
Camping Municipal du Lac Chemillé ✶✶
☎ 47.92.77.83
100 places, 15 Apr-30 Sep

THE LOIRE

lumière productions in August, was bought in the 19th century by Talleyrand, foreign minister to Napoléon. It was here that eminent overseas visitors were received in sumptuous luxury. It is still a beautiful place to visit with formal gardens, an animal park and, curiously, a vintage car museum.
Leisure
Château Montrésor open daily for guided visits, Apr-Oct ☎ 47.92.60.04; Château de Valençay open daily ☎ 54.00.10.66
Fishing Category 2 fishing on the Indrois.
Watersports Facilities for sailing, windsurfing, pedalo hire and bathing at the lake at Chemillé, just to the west.

SLIPPING OVER THE BORDER   *into Pays de la Loire*

MONTREUIL-BELLAY
Map ref. 127 F4
Pop 4,000
Saumur 16 km
Tours 85 km
Blois 143 km
Orléans 200 km
Paris 302 km
🛈 la Mairie
☎ 41.52.33.86
🛈 place des Ormeaux
☎ 41.52.32.39
Summer only

Small fortified town on a rocky spur between Anjou and Poitou, Montreuil-Bellay is delightfully unspoilt. Part medieval, part Renaissance, the château rises from the River Thouët.
Leisure
Aquarium More than 400 of the region's fish species on show. Open daily, Jul-Aug ☎ 41.52.35.90
Château Closed Tues ☎ 41.52.33.06
Cycling For local hire, enquire at the Tourist Office.
Fishing Category 1 fishing on the Thouët and its tributary, the Dive.
Golf See Chinon.
Wine Numerous outlets offer dégustations.
Zoo Open all year, at Doué-la-Fontaine to the north-west.

Hotel
Splendid Hôtel **
rue du Dr. Gaudrez
☎ 41.52.30.21
(and restaurant)

Camping
Airôtel les Nobis ***
☎ 41.52.33.66
165 places, Apr-Sep

Youth Hostel
La Roussillière
☎ 41.52.30.99
open all year

Restaurant
Hostellerie de la Porte Saint-Jean *
rue Nationale
☎ 41.52.30.41

MONTRICHARD
Map ref. 130 C3
Pop 4,000
Blois 34 km
Tours 41 km
Orléans 90 km
Paris 215 km
🛈 la Mairie
☎ 54.32.00.46
🛈 rue du Pont
☎ 54.32.05.10
Summer only

A pleasant little riverside town whose medieval walls, half-timbered houses and old bridge are dominated by the massive keep dating from 1010, once again the work of the tirelessly warring Count d'Anjou, Foulques Nerra. Troglodyte caves providing the exact level of humidity required for the storage of wine and the cultivation of mushrooms are also evident, and there are many well-known châteaux to visit in the area. Particularly worth searching out is the **Château de Gué-Péan**, quite extraordinarily beautiful.
Leisure
Château Château de Gué-Péan, 13 km east at Monthou-sur-Cher, is open daily (in summer) ☎ 54.71.43.01
Fishing Category 2 fishing on the Cher.
Riding Centre Equestre de Château.
Wine Tastings and cellar tours at Distillerie 'Fraise-d'Or', 62 route de Tours, Chissay-en-Touraine ☎ 54.32.32.05; also Caves Monmousseau, 71 rue de Vierzon, Montrichard ☎ 54.32.07.04
Watersports Beach for river bathing and good sports facilities at the Club Nautique de la Vallée du Cher.

Hotels
Hôtel Bellevue ***
quai du Cher
☎ 54.32.06.17
(and restaurant)
Hôtel la Tête Noire ***
rue de Tours
☎ 54.32.05.55
(and restaurant)

Camping
Municipal de l'Etourneau **
☎ 54.32.10.16
120 places

SLIPPING OVER THE BORDER
into Pays de la Loire

MONTSOREAU
Map ref. 127 E6
Pop 500
Chinon 20 km
Tours 62 km
Blois 121 km
Orléans 178 km
Paris 287 km
🛈 la Mairie,
place des
Diligences
☎ 41.51.70.15
🛈 avenue de
la Loire
☎ 41.51.70.22
Summer only

The magnificent 15th-century château fortress overlooks, and in fact has its foundations in, the mighty Loire. Set on the raised riverside bank, the carved-out troglodyte dwellings are much in evidence here as are the windmills and ancient houses which make up this tiny community. In summer the river is busy with those enjoying a variety of watersports activities. In the celebrated Coteaux du Saumurois vineyard area, there are liberal opportunities for *dégustations,* and this is also an important mushroom cultivation centre.

Close by in a single abbey, **Fontevraud l'Abbaye**, the English Angevin dynasty has left the bones of two of its kings, Henry II and his son Richard the Lionheart, and of two queens, Isabelle of Angoulême, wife of King John and Eleanor of Aquitaine. Eleanor, the wife of Henry and mother of Richard, was abbess here. Other features of this impressive 12th-century building are the cloisters, refectory and octagonal kitchen.

Hotels
Hôtel le Bussy **
Diane de Méridor
☎ 41.51.70.18
(and restaurant)
Hôtel de la Loire *
avenue la Loire
☎ 41.51.70.06
(and restaurant)

Camping
Municipal de l'Isle Verte **
☎ 41.51.76.60
160 places, May-Sep

Restaurant
Le Chapitre
quai Alexandre Dumas
☎ 41.51.75.33

INSIDE A CAVE DWELLING

Leisure
Château Mostly medieval with a Renaissance staircase, it now houses the Musée des Goums, Moroccan recruits to the French cavalry; closed Tues
☎ 41.51.70.25
Fishing Category 2 fishing in the Loire.
Golf See Chinon.
Museum Honouring the mushroom is the Musée du Champignon, route de Saumur; Mar-Nov.
Naturism A naturist centre ideally situated for visiting the châteaux, Bois de la Herpinière, Turquant ☎ 41.51.74.81
Watersports River bathing, canoeing and water-skiing from a beach here. Rowing and windsurfing tuition is available at weekends for beginners, Jun-Aug; enquire at the Tourist Office.

OLIVET

Map ref. 123 C4
Pop 15,000
Orléans 4 km
Blois 60 km
Tours 120 km
Paris 129 km
🛈 rue de
Général-de-Gaulle
☎ 38.63.49.68

Less than a stone's throw from the metropolis of Orléans, Olivet is a riverside town where the serene beauty of the River Loiret can best be appreciated by *bateau-mouche* water-bus trips. Sharing the river with swans, canoeists and rowers, a handful of old waterside mills will be encountered, evidence of past activities. Just to the east, at **Orléans-la-Source**, the River Loiret rises and a beautiful Parc Floral or botanical garden has been created around it. Each season brings its own reward: thousands of bulbs in spring, followed by azaleas, rhododendrons, over 600 varieties of irises, and roses, with a summer showing of masses of geraniums, chrysanthemums, begonias and petunias. Glorious trees, pink flamingos, emus and farm animals complete the picture.
The forested Sologne lies due south and of prime interest en route to the area is

Hotels
Hôtel Auberge les Quatre Saisons ***
351 rue de la Reine Blanche
☎ 38.66.14.30
(and ****restaurant)
Hôtel Climat de France **
20 route de Bourges
☎ 38.69.20.55
(and restaurant)
Hôtel le Plissay **
66 allée des Villas
☎ 38.66.02.12
Hôtel Resthotel-Primevère **
410 rue d'Artois
☎ 38.76.45.45
(and restaurant)
Hôtel le Rivage **
rue de la Reine Blanche
☎ 38.66.02.93
(and ***restaurant)

Camping
Municipal **
rue du Pont Bouchet
☎ 38.63.53.94
80 places

Restaurant
Madagascar ***
rue de la Reine Blanche
☎ 38.66.12.58

BANKS OF THE LOIRET, AT OLIVET

JOAN OF ARC (c. 1412-31)

At the beginning of the 15th century France's fortunes in her century-old struggle for supremacy against England were at their lowest. The effect of the catastrophic defeat at Agincourt by Henry V still hung over the French. Charles VII, heir to the mad king Charles VI, languished in Bourges unable to extricate himself from the intrigues of his own Court where apathy and despondency prevailed. Still uncrowned and full of self-doubt as to his legitimacy, Charles was encircled by the English and Burgundian alliance who referred to him mockingly as 'the King of Bourges', a humiliating jibe.

It was at this moment that there emerged one of the most extraordinary figures in French history. Joan of Arc, a young peasant girl from Domrémy in Lorraine, full of visions of herself as the saviour of France, travelled to Chinon to seek an audience with Charles. The uncrowned king hid amongst his courtiers but was immediately recognised as the Dauphin by the young Joan. Charles was struck by her innocence and passion for his cause and gave her men and arms. Joan raised the siege of Orléans, recaptured Jargeau and Beaugency from the English and then crushed the English counter-attack at Patay. These successes in the summer of 1429 persuaded Charles of his right and he was crowned at Rheims.

The tide of war now turned in the French king's favour. Joan's personal success however was short-lived. She was captured by the Burgundians at Compiègne and sold to the English. A trial at Rouen followed and Joan was condemned to death as a witch and burnt at the stake. The judgment against her was reversed in 1456.

The French army's success may have been due to their effective use of artillery, but the shepherdess from Lorraine revived French patriotism. It was no accident that during the Second World War, after the fall of France to the Nazis, de Gaulle chose the cross of Lorraine as the symbol of the Free French resistance movement. Joan, often referred to as the Maid of Orléans, was canonized in 1920.

the 17th-century **Château de la Ferté-St-Aubin**, a visit to which also includes a deer park, farm animals and stables.

Leisure
Boat Trips By bateau-mouche *along the River Loiret, daily Apr-Nov* ☎ 38.66.12.58
Château Open daily, Mar-Nov ☎ 38.76.52.72
Fishing Category 2 fishing on the Loiret.
Golf See Beaugency and Orléans.
Wine Tastings and cellar tours at Covifruit, 613 rue du Pressoir-Tonneau ☎ 38.63.40.20

ORLEANS
Map ref. 123 C4
Pop 105,000
Blois 58 km
Tours 118 km
Paris 125 km
🛈 place Albert Ier
☎ 38.53.05.95

La Pucelle d'Orléans or the Maid of Orléans, patron saint of France, is a figure known throughout the world. Joan of Arc's role in the history of Orléans and of France is recorded in the stained glass of the Gothic cathedral of Ste-Croix, in an equestrian statue in place Martroi and another bronze outside the fine Renaissance Hôtel Groslot, now the Town Hall. Since her courageous liberation of the city from the English in 1429, the feat has been celebrated annually on 7-8 May, and in great style, a mix of civil, military and religious processions.

As the capital of the Centre region, the city is foremost an industrial, commercial and cultural centre with a large university, art gallery and museums and excellent shopping and dining. Despite massive bomb damage in the last war, there do exist some early buildings in the old quarter of the city, though Joan of Arc's house is a replica. Guided walking tours are available, or alternatively pre-recorded tapes to follow at your own pace can be hired.

Three different motoring routes can be followed from the city: *la Vallée des Rois du Val de Loire* with thirty-two monuments; *les Hauts Dignitaires de la Seine à la Loire* with twelve châteaux; and the *Route Jacques-Coeur* with fourteen châteaux. Itineraries for these are available from the Tourist Office.

Leisure
Art Musée des Beaux Arts, place Ste-Croix, near the cathedral, has a good collection of French and foreign schools. Open daily, except Tues ☎ 38.53.39.22
Cycling Cycles for hire from the SNCF station.
Fishing Category 2 fishing on the Loire, Loiret and canal.
Golf 18-hole private course at Golf de la Plaine, Marcilly-en-Villette, 45240 La Ferté-Saint-Aubin ☎ 38.76.11.73; see also Beaugency.
Guided Tours Themed walking tours of the centre operate on Wed and Sun afternoons, and tape recordings can also be hired. Also available are tours in a small tourist train, or, for a spectacular bird's eye view of the area, by light aircraft. Enquire at the Tourist Office for bookings.
Loisirs Accueil Cycling holiday consisting of seven-day round tour of La Vallée des

Hotels
Hôtel d'Arc ★★★
37 rue de la République
☎ 38.53.10.94
Hôtel les Cèdres ★★★
17 rue Maréchal Foch
☎ 38.62.22.92
Hôtel Chéops ★★★
quai de la Madeleine
☎ 38.43.92.92
Hôtel d'Orléans ★★★
6 rue Adolphe Crespin
☎ 38.53.35.34
Hôtel le Saint Aignan ★★★
place Gambetta
☎ 38.53.15.35
Hôtel Sofitel ★★★
44 quai Barentin
☎ 38.62.17.39 (and restaurant)
Hôtel Terminus ★★★
40 rue de la République
☎ 38.53.24.64

Restaurants
Les Antiquaires ★★★★
2 rue au Lin
☎ 38.53.52.35
La Crémaillère ★★★★
34 rue Notre Dame de Recouvrance
☎ 38.53.49.17
L'Ami Stephane ★★
rue Ste-Catherine
☎ 38.53.38.97

JOAN OF ARC, ORLEANS

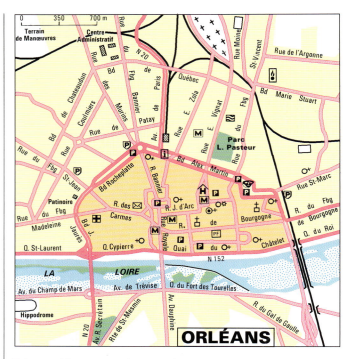

Rois *past châteaux, manor houses and through lovely countryside. Operates throughout the year and the price of 2,300FF per person includes * or ** hotel accommodation, hire of cycle, onward transport of luggage and detailed itinerary. Bookable through Loisirs Accueil Loiret (address on page 27).*
Museum *Fine Gallo-Roman bronzes are a particular feature of the Musée Archéologique et Historique d'Orléans, Hôtel Cabu, place Abbé Desnoyers* ☎ *38.53.92.22 closed Tues.*
Riding *Les Ecuries du Val de Loire, Domaine de Barbereau* ☎ *38.41.00.30*

A town fit for a Cardinal, Richelieu was created in the early 17th century in memory of its founder, one of France's premier statesmen.
Prime Minister to Louis XIII, Cardinal Richelieu had his own vast palace nearby but required a suitable environment in which to house his court. Work started on the planned town in 1631 to the designs of the king's architect, Jacques Lemercier, and is a model of urban design quite perfect in its symmetry. Based on a rectangular grid layout, the whole is walled and moated and entered by roofed gateways leading into the Grande-Rue, a straight avenue lined with identical white stone, slate-roofed mansions, each with its own carriage entrance. Away from the centre, terraces of smaller houses provide accommodation for those of lesser rank. The Cardinal's own palace was demolished in the 19th century, though

RICHELIEU
Map ref. 136 A2
Pop 2,000
Tours 59 km
Blois 118 km
Orléans 175 km
Paris 287 km
🛈 la Mairie
☎ 47.58.10.13
☎ 47.58.13.62
Summer only

Hotel
Hôtel Puits Doré **
24 place du Marché
☎ 47.58.10.59
(and restaurant)

Camping
Municipal **
route de Châtellerault
☎ 47.58.10.13
33 places

the park which remains, now owned by the University of Paris, is a beautiful place in which to wander.
Leisure
Golf See Chinon.
Guided Tours Town tours on request from the Tourist Office.
Steam Train Short trips on a 1920s steam train between Richelieu, Champigny-sur-Veude and Chinon through the Touraine countryside; weekends, May-Sep. Enquire at the Tourist Office.

SLIPPING OVER THE BORDER   into Poitou-Charentes

LA ROCHE-POSAY
Map ref. 137 D5
Pop 2,000
Poitiers 49 km
Tours 77 km
Blois 114 km
Orléans 169 km
Paris 294 km
🛈 cours Pasteur
☎ 49.86.20.37

A small picturesque spa town set on a hill by the ruins of a 12th-century keep, with the winding River Gartempe and the modern spa centre on a plateau at the foot. The large number of *curistes* or 'patients' who stay for periods of up to three weeks means that the accommodation, sporting and leisure facilities are good for a small town, with fishing, a racecourse and greyhound track, excellent golf course and a casino. The two spa centres are reputed for their beneficial effects on people suffering from skin diseases and a quarter of those treated here are young children.
In one direction lies the châteaux country of the Loire whilst to the west is the architecturally exciting city of Poitiers. If you are looking for something completely different, popular with adults and children alike is the newly-created Futuroscope, a unique amusement park complex where all the senses are treated to unusual experiences – a fascinating world of discovery amidst the scientific and futuristic attractions.
Leisure
Casino Open all year ☎ 49.86.20.10
Fishing Category 2 fishing on the Creuse and Gartempe rivers.
Fitness Centre Combining hotel accommodation and water treatment therapy with golf, tennis, gymnastics and aerobics, on a weekly or weekend basis. Open May-Oct, contact Espace Mélusine, Parc Thermal, 86270 La Roche-Posay ☎ 49.86.20.21
Futuroscope Near Poitiers at Jaunay-Clan ☎ 49.62.30.20 open daily, closed Mon and Tues out of season, except public holidays.
Golf 18-hole private hilly, woodland course at Golf de Châtelleraudais, Parc du Connétable, 86270 La Roche-Posay ☎ 49.86.20.21
Riding La Gatinière Equitation, route de Lésigny ☎ 49.86.18.35
Spa Skin diseases treated at Thermes Saint-Roch, open all year ☎ 49.86.21.03 and Thermes du Connétable, Apr-Oct ☎ 49.86.20.21
Walking Accompanied group walks organized by the Tourist Office, Apr-Oct.

Hotels
Hôtel Thermal Saint-Roch ✱✱✱
cours Pasteur
☎ 49.86.21.03
(and restaurant)
Hôtel de l'Esplanade ✱✱
37 cours Pasteur
☎ 49.86.20.48
(and restaurant)
Hôtel de l'Europe ✱✱
19 avenue des Fontaines
☎ 49.86.21.81

Camping
Le Riveau ✱✱✱
☎ 49.86.21.23
200 places, Mar-Oct

THE KINEMAX: FUTUROSCOPE PARK

ROMORANTIN-LANTHENAY
Map ref. 132 C1
Pop 19,000
Blois 43 km
Orléans 69 km
Tours 90 km
Paris 194 km
🛈 place de la Paix
☎ 54.76.43.89

A large and pleasant market town at the centre of the **Sologne** country of heathland, woods and lakes in a loop of the Loire below Orléans. Much of this land is private so is not ideal for walkers, but there is excellent fishing in the River Sauldre which flows through the old town with its ancient houses and gardens, and lovely views of the 15th-century Château du Moulin from the several bridges which cross the river.

An ideal centre for excursions to the châteaux of the Loire, with Cheverny only 28 km, Beauregard 30 km and Chambord 38 km away, and many others on the *François 1er Route* from Sologne to Berry. Indoor and outdoor swimming pools, a skating rink and an interesting museum add to the diversions here.

Leisure
Cycling Cycles for hire from the SNCF station.
Fishing Category 2 fishing on the Sauldre.
Golf Flat narrow 9-hole private course at Golf de Salbris, Château de Rivaulde, 41300 Salbris ☎ 54.97.21.85
Museum Musée de Sologne, Hôtel de Ville ☎ 54.76.07.06

Hotels
Grand Hôtel du Lion d'Or ***
69 rue Georges Clémenceau
☎ 54.76.00.28
(and **** restaurant)
Hôtel Auberge de Lanthenay **
place de l'Eglise
☎ 54.76.09.19
(and restaurant)
Hôtel le Colombier **
10 place du Vieux Marché
☎ 54.76.12.76
(and *** restaurant)
Hôtel d'Orléans **
place du Général de Gaulle
☎ 54.76.01.65
(and *** restaurant)

Camping
Tournefeuille ****
rue Long Eaton
☎ 54.76.16.60
500 places

Restaurant
La Cabrière **
avenue de Villefranche
☎ 54.76.38.94

ST-AMAND MONTROND
Map ref. 141 D6
Pop 12,000
Bourges 44 km
Blois 147 km
Tours 180 km
Orléans 151 km
Paris 270 km
🛈 place de la République
☎ 48.96.16.86

Designated a *station verte* or country holiday resort, St-Amand is a lively and pleasant town amidst the hilly wooded countryside of **Boischaut** with a number of interesting old buildings at its heart. Gold jewellery-making has been a prime industry in the area for some time and St-Amand is now the second most important assaying office in France.

On the *Route Jacques Coeur* which takes the traveller away from the beaten track in search of less well-known châteaux and historic monuments, of particular interest locally are: the **Abbaye de Noirlac** 4 km away, a showpiece of medieval monastic architecture; the beautiful Renaissance **Château Meillant**, 7 km; the interesting medieval and Renaissance mix of **Ainay-le-Vieil**, 11 km, with its rose gardens; the riverside fortifications and town of **Dun-sur-Auron**, 20 km; and the medieval fortress of **Culan**, 23 km. The exact

Hotels
Hôtel la Croix d'Or **
28 rue du 14 juillet
☎ 48.96.09.41
(and restaurant)
Hôtel le Noirlac **
route de Bourges
☎ 48.96.80.80
(and restaurant)
Hôtel la Poste **
rue Docteur Vallet
☎ 48.96.27.14
(and restaurant)

Camping
Municipal de la Roche **
☎ 48.96.09.36
100 places

MEILLANT CHATEAU

geographical centre of France has been calculated as being at the small village of **Vesdun** to the south.
Leisure
Bathing River bathing in the Cher.
Cycling Cycles for hire from the SNCF station.

Restaurant
Le Boeuf Couronné **
86 rue Juranville
☎ 48.96.42.72

JACQUES COEUR (1400-1456)
A wealthy banker and merchant from Bourges, Jacques Coeur was responsible for the skilful reorganization of the French taxation system with which to finance the continued war against the English. Under Charles VII he was made responsible too for the royal finances, something he managed with such success that it enabled a huge building programme of palaces and châteaux to go ahead, particularly in the Loire valley.

When the king's mistress, **Agnès Sorel**, died in mysterious circumstances, Coeur came under suspicion. Falsely accused of her poisoning, he was forced to flee France, unable to live in the magnificent Palais Jacques Coeur in Bourges which he had commissioned, and finally dying far away on a Greek island.

Today, the visitor can follow the motoring itinerary *Route Jacques Coeur* which passes through the *départements* of Loiret and Cher, the 17 châteaux en route all having medieval associations.

Route Jacques Coeur
La Bussière, Gien, Argent, Blancafort, Aubigny-sur-Nère, La Verrerie, Boucard, La Chapelle-d'Angillon, Maupas, Menetou-Salon, Bourges, Jussy-Champagne, Dun-sur-Auron, Meillant, Abbaye de Noirlac, Ainay-le-Vieil and Culan.
Details are available from the Tourist Office in St-Amand and from the Comité Départemental du Tourisme, Hôtel du Département, 10 rue de la Chappe, 18014 Bourges ☎ 48.70.71.72

Fishing Category 2 fishing on the Cher and Marmande rivers, also the Canal de Berry.
Loisirs Accueil Accompanied group canoeing trip on the River Cher from St-Amand to Preuilly. Priced for six days at 1,495FF per person from sixteen yrs upwards, cost includes equipment, supervisor, onward transport of luggage and campsite accommodation. Details from Loisirs Accueil Cher (address on page 27).
Watersports Sailing on the Etang de Goule, 20 km away, and the very popular lake at Sidiailles, 30 km.

SANCERRE
Map ref. 135 C4
Pop 3,000
Bourges 53 km
Orléans 113 km
Blois 144 km
Tours 189 km
Paris 202 km
🅱 la Mairie
☎ 48.54.00.26
🅱 Nouvelle Place
☎ 48.54.08.21
Summer only

Another *station verte*, or rural location with tourist 'resort' status, whose popularity is easy to appreciate. From its hilltop position this little town oversees the cultivation of the grape and the goat – its hillside vineyards producing notable dry white wines, and from the farms of its neighbouring village, the *crottins de Chavignol*, goats' cheeses of some considerable merit.

Panoramic views across the peaceful landscape from the ruined ramparts of Porte César at the top of the town seem to belie the town's turbulent history. At the centre of the fighting during the Hundred Years' War with the English, it was later besieged several times because of its Protestant status. In 1573, the people held out for seven months until the point of starvation, accounts relating how they were forced to eat the parchment of their maps and manuscripts mixed with water.

Hotels
Hôtel Panoramic **
rempart des Augustins
☎ 48.54.22.44
(and restaurant)
Hôtel du Rempart **
rempart des Dames
☎ 48.54.10.18
(and restaurant)
Hôtel le Saint-Martin **
rue Saint-Martin
☎ 48.54.21.11
(and restaurant)

Camping
Camping René Foltzer **
Saint-Thibault
☎ 48.54.04.67
50 places

A far cry from those days, today's 'invaders' enjoy the produce of the region in much greater comfort. Good restaurants and sporting facilities include the new golf course on the banks of the Loire with the Sancerrois hills in the background.

Restaurant
Tasse d'Argent ★★★
rempart des Augustins
☎ 48.54.01.44

GRAPE PICKING AT SANCERRE

Leisure
Bathing River bathing from a sandy beach close by at St-Thibault-sur-Loire. There is also a pleasure boat base here.
Fishing Category 2 fishing on the Loire, also the Canal Latéral.
Golf 18-hole course at Golf du Sancerrois, Saint-Thibault Saint-Satur, 18300 Sancerre ☎ 48.54.11.22
Nuclear Power Station The two huge cooling towers at Belleville-sur-Loire, 25 km north, dominate the installation on the left bank of the Loire. Guided visits by prior appointment, with at least three weeks' notice, by applying to Electricité de France, Centrale de Belleville-sur-Loire, BP 11, 18240 Léré ☎ 48.54.50.92. Foreign visitors must present their passports.
Wine Tastings and cellar tours at Cave de la Cresle, Domaine Laporte ☎ 48.54.04.07

SLIPPING OVER THE BORDER *into Pays de la Loire*

SAUMUR
Map ref. 127 D5
Pop 34,000
Angers 50 km
Tours 69 km
Blois 127 km
Orléans 189 km
Paris 287 km
🛈 25 rue Beaurepaire
☎ 41.51.03.06

Unique in France, and renowned worldwide for its Cadre Noir cavalry school, the old equestrian traditions are still maintained at the National Riding School. Noted also for the white wine produced in the surrounding vineyards, Saumur is a beautiful château town, twinned with the equally impressive Warwick in England, with some fine stone buildings and a massive bridge across the Loire. Ideal as a base for exploring the great and innumerable châteaux in the region.

Leisure
Cavalry School Founded in 1766 and situated on the outskirts of the town at Terrefort, the Cadre Noir Cavalry School is open for schooling courses for French and foreign students. Enquire at the Tourist Office for dates of forthcoming displays.
Château Now housing two museums: the

Hotels
Hôtel Anne d'Anjou ★★★
32 quai Mayaud
☎ 41.67.30.30
Loire Hôtel ★★★
rue du Vieux Pont
☎ 41.67.22.42
(and restaurant)
Campanile ★★
rond-point de Bournan
☎ 41.50.14.40
(and restaurant)
Hôtel Le Chéops ★★
avenue des Fusiliers, St-Lambert-des-Levées
☎ 41.67.17.18 (and restaurant)
Le Clos des Bénédictins ★★
St-Hilaire-St-Florent
☎ 41.67.28.48
(and restaurant)

Musée des Arts décoratifs and the Musée du Cheval ☎ 41.51.30.46
Cycling Cycles for hire from the SNCF station.
Fishing Category 2 fishing on the Loire.
Golf See Angers and Chinon.
Riding Centre de Tourisme Equestre, La

SAUMUR CHATEAU

Métairie, Trèves-Cunault ☎ 41.67.92.43; also Pony-Club, boulevard de la Marne ☎ 41.50.19.21
Tradition Festival d'Anjou at the end of July includes displays by the Cadre Noir.
Watersports Club Nautique, quai du Maronnier ☎ 41.67.36.40
Wine Wine Fair, second week in Feb; the Maison du Vin de Saumur, 25 rue Beaurepaire ☎ 41.51.16.40 can provide itineraries and interesting reading matter on the subject.

Hôtel de Londres **
rue d'Orléans
☎ 41.51.23.98

Camping
Camping de Chantepie la Croix ****
St-Hilaire-St-Florent
☎ 41.67.95.34
150 places, May-Sep
L'Ile d'Offard ***
rue de Verden
☎ 41.67.45.00
270 places, open all year

Youth Hostel
Centre International de Séjour
Ile d'Offard
rue de Verden
☎ 41.67.45.00
open all year

Restaurants
L'Escargot **
30 rue du Maréchal Leclerc
☎ 41.51.20.88
Le Gambetta **
12 rue Gambetta
☎ 41.67.66.66

SULLY-SUR-LOIRE
Map ref. 124 D2
Pop 6,000
Orléans 43 km
Blois 94 km
Paris 142 km
Tours 155 km
🛈 place de Gaulle
☎ 38.36.23.70

One of the great moated châteaux of the Loire valley, the imposing medieval fortress faces quiet parkland. Owned in the early 17th century by the brilliant statesman and financial secretary to the king, Maximilien de Béthune, Duke of Sully, who was responsible for the additions and embellishments which created a domestic residence within the original walls. Of particular note, though from the earlier 14th-century building, is the huge oak ceiling in the form of an upturned ship's hull.
Numerous excursions are possible throughout the area while local diversions include river bathing from the small beach and play area close to the château, canoeing and riding.
Leisure
Château Open daily, Mar-Nov; classical music festival held in the château courtyard, Jun-Jul ☎ 38.36.25.60
Fishing Category 2 fishing on the Loire, in choice spots along the Sange river and in Les Douves, the château's moated waters.
Golf 18-hole private course at Golf Club de Sully, L'Ousseau-Viglain, 45600 Sully-sur-Loire ☎ 38.36.52.08
Loisirs Accueil Week-long riding holidays throughout the year operate from Sat-Sat and consist of practical lessons in horse-management, outings, jump classes and visits to other stables and establishments

Hotels
Hôtel le Concorde **
1 rue Porte de Sologne
☎ 38.36.24.44
(and restaurant)
Hostellerie du Grand Sully **
boulevard du Champ de Foire
☎ 38.36.27.56
(and restaurant)
Hôtel du Pont du Sologne **
rue Porte de Sologne
☎ 38.36.26.34
(and restaurant)
Hôtel la Poste **
11 rue de Faubourg Saint Germain
☎ 38.36.26.22
(and *** restaurant)

Camping
Municipal **
☎ 38.36.23.93
133 places

Restaurant
L'Esplanade **
place Pilier
☎ 38.36.20.83

of interest to horse-lovers. The price of 1,200FF per person includes meals and accommodation at the stables which are situated near to the golf course at Viglain, and experienced instruction. Contact Loisirs Accueil Loiret for details of this and other riding holidays. Also, for swimmers only, day canoeing and kayaking trips on waters suited to your ability (calm or lively), under qualified instruction. Cost is 150FF per day; more for five-day courses in July and Aug, and trips start from a base between Sully and Beaugency. Contact Loisirs Accueil Loiret for details (address on page 27).
Riding Centre Hippique, Domaine de l'Arlantoy ☎ 38.36.23.52

SULLY-SUR-LOIRE CHATEAU

TOURS
Map ref. 129 C5
Pop 136,000
Blois 61 km
Angers 108 km
Orléans 118 km
Paris 228 km
🅸 place Maréchal-Leclerc
☎ 47.05.58.08

Tours, the metropolis on the Loire near its junction with the Cher, is at the heart of what was once exclusively agricultural land but which has now embraced electronics, pharmaceuticals, plastics and the service industries. A centre for higher education, its university has 12,000 students, and there are 3,000 foreign students of the French language based here.

Between the 13th and 15th centuries, the Château Royal de Tours was the residence of the French Valois monarchs, later becoming a military barracks until, after World War II, it was split into three museums. Great restoration work began in 1970 and the area around the place Plumereau, the old quarter of the city near the university, came to new life with pedestrian precincts, small courtyards of 15th-century timbered houses and narrow streets leading to quiet gardens.

Hotels
Hôtel Bardet ****
57 rue Groisons
☎ 47.41.41.11
(and **** restaurant)
Hôtel Alliance ***
292 avenue de Grammont
☎ 47.28.00.80
(and restaurant)
Videotel le Bordeaux ***
3 place Maréchal Leclerc
☎ 47.05.40.32
(and restaurant)
Central Hôtel ***
21 rue Berthelot
☎ 47.05.46.44
Grand Hôtel ***
9 place Maréchal Leclerc
☎ 47.05.35.31
Hôtel Royal ***
65 avenue de Grammont
☎ 47.64.71.78

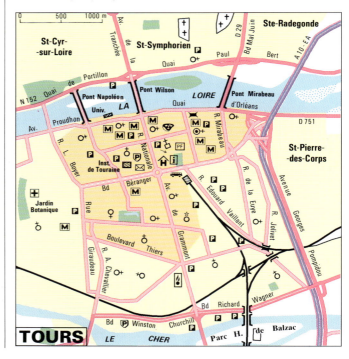

GAZETTEER

GARDEN OF LOVE (VILLANDRY)

Dating from 1536, this is the last of the great Renaissance châteaux to be built along the banks of the Loire. Villandry was the residence of Jean le Breton, Secretary of State to François I. Today, however, it is not so much the building as its fabulous terraced gardens both of flowers and of vegetables which particularly attract visitors.

The property was acquired early this century by Dr Joachim de Carvallo, founder of the *Demeure Historique* association, and it was on his instruction that the gardens, which had undergone some modification and landscaping according to the current fashion of the English country-house in the previous century, were restored to their original design. They now present the richly formal style traditional to 16th-century France, with Villandry the only authentic garden of its type.

The gardens are laid out on three tiers: *le jardin d'eau* or water garden, *le jardin d'ornement* or ornamental garden and *le potager* or kitchen garden. It is possible to view them all from the balustraded château terraces with the River Cher and valley beyond, even better to see them from the air.

Paths run between the strict square-shaped herb gardens, miniature knee-high hedges, flowers in geometrical patterns on beds of medicinal plants. The Garden of Love is a delight, the intricately sculpted shapes of the clipped boxwood hedges evoking the four faces of Love: *tragique*, represented by daggers and double-edged swords; *volage*, by fans and letters; *tendre* by masks and hearts; and *passionné* by broken hearts. The water garden is overlooked by stilt hedges, that is clipped hedges with bare trunks revealed, and consists of fountains, cascades, a moat and a huge ornamental lake at the centre.

Situated 15 km west of Tours, 10 km from Azay-le-Rideau, the gardens are open daily throughout the year. The château is open 15 Mar-11 Nov ☎ 47.50.02.09, with guided tours which include an impressive slide show revealing the changing beauty of the gardens throughout the seasons.

For a stunning view of the châteaux from the air, there are helicopter flights passing over Villandry, Langeais, Ussé, Chinon, Azay-le-Rideau, Chenonceau, Cheverny, Chambord, Ménars, Blois, Chaumont and Amboise. Bookable through Loisirs Accueil Indre-et-Loire, 38 rue Augustin-Fresnel, BP 139, 37171 Chambray-lès-Tours ☎ 47.48.37.27, the tours depart from the aerodrome at Amboise-Dierre for a round trip lasting 1 hr 30 mins and costing 8,220FF (min. 4 passengers).

Tours holds a number of concerts and exhibitions during the year, principally perhaps the Touraine Music Festival, held at the Grange de Meslay, a 13th-century tithe barn, at the end of June. Above all Tours is ideally situated as a centre for visits to the Loire valley châteaux which encircle it (Chinon, Azay-le-Rideau, Amboise, Chenconceau, Cheverny, Chambord and Blois), by road or, for a bird's eye view, from the air by helicopter and balloon.

Leisure
Cycling Cycles for hire from the SNCF station.
Golf 18-hole private course at Golf de Touraine, Château de la Touche, 37510 Joué-les-Tours ☎ 47.53.20.28; and 18-hole course at Golf de l'Ardrée, St-Antoine-du-Rocher, 37360 Neuillé-Pont-Pierre ☎ 47.56.77.38. New 9-hole public course at Golf du Val de l'Indre, Parc du Château de Villedieu, Villedieu-sur-Indre ☎ 54.26.59.44
Guided Tours Tours by bus with stops for visits available from the Tourist Office.
Loisirs Accueil Helicopter and light aircraft flights over the châteaux, bookable through Loisirs Accueil Indre-et-Loire (address on page 27). Also bookable are tennis courses at the Club de Tours.
Medieval suppers Dine in authentic surroundings – châteaux, wine cellars, abbeys, etc., with costumed waitressing,

Hôtel Univers ★★★
5 boulevard Heurteloup
☎ 47.05.37.12
(and restaurant)
Hôtel Akilene ★★
22 rue du Grand Marché
☎ 47.61.46.04
(and restaurant)
Hôtel Arcade ★★
1 rue G. Claude
☎ 47.61.44.44
(and restaurant)
Hôtel Balzac ★★
47 rue de la Scellerie
☎ 47.05.40.87

Camping
Municipal Edouard Péron ★★
☎ 47.54.11.11
62 places

Youth Hostel
Parc de Grammont
☎ 47.25.14.45
open all year

Restaurants
Barrier ★★★★
101 avenue de la Tranchée
☎ 47.54.20.39
La Roche le Roy ★★★★
55 route de St-Avertin
☎ 47.27.22.00

THE LOIRE AT TOURS

musicians and entertainment. Organized by Comedia Nova, 10 bis rue Racine ☎ 47.20.92.02
Museums French and foreign art to the present day at Musée des Beaux Arts, place François Sicard ☎ 47.05.68.73; three museums within the château cover the history of the Touraine, a tropical aquarium and a historical presentation of the city of Tours.
Riding Centre Equestre La Martinière, Les Savonnières ☎ 47.50.04.46
Wine Musée des Vins de Touraine, rue Nationale, museum and cellars ☎ 47.61.07.93 closed Tues.

La Rôtisserie Tourangelle ****
23 rue du Commerce
☎ 47.05.71.21

VENDOME
Map ref. 120 D3
Pop 18,000
Blois 32 km
Tours 57 km
Orléans 75 km
Paris 171 km
🖪 47/19 rue Poterie
☎ 54.77.05.07

The Loir winds sinuously through this charming town, branching off to form various tiny islands connected by bridges, across which shoppers walk to rest in quiet parks or to picnic in the shade of ancient trees. There are also attractive pedestrian walkways, like the rue du Change where the wares of the shops spill out through the doors, and surprises, like the huge waterwheel turning behind glass in the Vieux Moulin restaurant in the cours du Moulin Perrin. Surrounded by gently rolling farmland, there are lovely views from the ruined château at the top of the town.
Leisure
Château Son-et-lumière summer productions amongst the ruins.
Cycling Cycles for hire from the SNCF station.
Golf See Beaugency and Blois.
Guided Tours Audio tapes for hire from the Tourist Office for walking tours.
Loisirs Accueil From a base at Savigny-sur-Braye, just to the north of Vendôme, accompanied horse-riding treks on a half-day or longer basis; overnight camping 350FF. Contact Loisirs Accueil Loir-et-Cher for details of these and other riding holidays (address on page 27).

Hotels
Hôtel Vendôme ***
15 faubourg Chartrain
☎ 54.77.02.88
(and restaurant)
Hôtel Capricorne **
boulevard de Trémault
☎ 54.80.27.00
(and restaurant)
Grand Hôtel Saint-Georges **
14 rue Poterie
☎ 54.77.25.42
(and *** restaurant)

Camping
Municipal des Grands Prés ***
☎ 54.77.00.27
600 places

Restaurants
Le Paris ***
1 rue Darreau
☎ 54.77.02.71
Chez Annette **
faubourg Chartrain
☎ 54.77.23.03

VIERZON
Map ref. 132 E3
Pop 35,000
Bourges 33 km
Blois 75 km
Orléans 80 km
Tours 115 km
Paris 205 km
🅘 place Thorez
☎ 48.75.20.03

Riding Pony Club de la Source, rue des Bigotteries ☎ 54.77.06.95
Walking Signposted footpaths through the Forêt d'Oratoire.
Watersports Sailing, windsurfing, fishing, etc on a stretch of water at Villiers-sur-Loir, to the north-west opposite Château Rochambeau.

Associated with the porcelain industry since the last century like its close neighbour, Mehun-sur-Yèvre, the town is now more heavily and variously industrialized.
Marking the confluence of the Cher and the Yèvre, parts of the town have remained attractive, notably its watery sections, the canalside wharves of the Canal de Berry connecting directly with the railway junction. There are traces too of 'vieux' Vierzon with some half-timbered houses in the narrow streets of the older quarters. The Gothic church of Notre-Dame has some notable stained glass and wood panelling.

Leisure
Fishing Category 2 fishing on the River Cher and Canal de Berry.
Golf See Romorantin-Lanthenay and Sancerre.

Hotels
Hôtel le Continental ***
avenue Edouard Vaillant
☎ 48.75.35.22
Hôtel Chalet de la Forêt **
avenue Edouard Vaillant
☎ 48.75.35.84
(and restaurant)
Hôtel Terminus et Bordeaux **
24 avenue Pierre Semard
☎ 48.75.00.46

Camping
Municipal de Bellon **
☎ 48.75.49.10
80 places

Youth Hostel
place de la République
☎ 48.75.30.62
open all year

Restaurant
Le Champêtre **
route de Tours
☎ 48.75.87.18

CELLAR AT VOUVRAY

VOUVRAY
Map ref. 129 C6
Pop 2,000
Tours 10 km
Blois 51 km
Orléans 108 km
Paris 231 km
🅘 la Mairie
☎ 47.52.70.48

Emerging from amongst the thousands of vines which cover the slopes of the surrounding countryside, this little town owes its renown to a great white wine of the same name. Roadside *dégustations* or tastings, and some memorable views over the Loire are possible at numerous locations all found within a short circuit of the town.

Leisure
Fishing Available with permit on the Cisse and Loire rivers.
Golf See Tours.
Wine Cellar visits at Cave Coopérative des Producteurs des Grands Vins, Vallée Coquette ☎ 47.52.75.03, open daily. The principal wine fairs are held on the last Sat in Jan and on 15 Aug.

Hotel
Auberge du Grand Vatel **
avenue Brûlé
☎ 47.52.70.32
(and restaurant)

Restaurant
Virage Gastronomique **
26 avenue Brûlé
☎ 47.52.70.02

PRACTICAL INFORMATION

TRAVEL INFORMATION

By car
The international road sign system operates in France. Driving is on the right-hand side of the road and it is important to remember to yield right-of-way to the right when emerging from a stationary position. The French motorway system is run by private enterprise and tolls are levied on all the *autoroutes à péage*. Service stations with full facilities are located every 25 km and there are also *aire de repos* or rest areas where motorists can break their journeys. In the event of a breakdown or accident on a motorway, contact the police by using the emergency telephones sited every 2 km in orange posts. If the car electrics have failed, place the hazard warning triangle 45 m behind your vehicle.

- Speed limits
  open road 90 kmph (55 mph)
  dual carriageways 110 kmph (68 mph)
  towns and cities 60 kmph (37 mph)
  motorways 130 kmph (80 mph)
  Paris ring roads 80 kmph (49 mph)
- Seat belts must be worn, by law.
- Helmets must be worn on motorcycles and motorbikes.

The traffic jams at the beginning and end of August, when the whole of France seems to be on the move, are best avoided. During this period alternative itineraries or *itinéraires bis* (sometimes just *Bis* for short) are signposted which take motorists away from the traditionally congested routes.

Up-to-date telephone information on road and traffic conditions in the region can be obtained from:
Circulation routière province
☎ 48.99.33.33
Inter service routes
☎ 48.94.33.33
3615 + autoroutes
3615 + iti (itinéraires)

Car hire
If you are considering hiring a vehicle while in France, car hire can be arranged locally by enquiring at the Tourist Office, or in advance by contacting any of the following international agencies.

Avis
☎ 081–848 8733
Budget
☎ 0442 232555
Europcar
☎ 081–950 5050
Hertz
☎ 081–679 1799

By air
Airports serving the Loire region are Châteauroux and Tours. All flights to France are handled by Air France, 158 New Bond Street, London W1Y 0AY
☎ 071–499 9511.

By sea
Cross-Channel ferries and hovercraft offer quick and cheap car and passenger crossings throughout the year. Brochures detailing crossings (some only operate during the summer months) and fares are available at travel agents nationwide.

By train
The French railway system is run by the Société Nationale des Chemins de fer Français, or SNCF for short, and is the largest rail network in western Europe. Details of fares, routes and special deals and reductions are available from principal British Rail Travel Centres and continental rail-appointed travel agents. Many stations offer car hire and over 240 of them also offer a cycle hire service. SNCF (French Railways), 179 Piccadilly, London W1V 0BA.

GENERAL INFORMATION

Banks
Open regular hours, Monday-Friday, 9 a.m.-12 noon and 2–4 p.m., though most will be open all day in Paris or regional capitals. Some will open on Saturday mornings too if that is market day, but stay closed on Mondays instead. Banks will not only close on, but also around, some public holidays – see National Holidays. This is known as *faire le pont*, literally 'bridging the gap'. In the case of banks, notices posted outside give advance warning.

Emergencies and Problems
There are two emergency phone numbers:

Police and Ambulance **17**   Fire **18**

In the event of sickness, *pharmacies* or chemists' shops can provide addresses of local doctors and the nearest hospital casualty department.

Amboise
Hôpital
☎ 47.23.33.33
Blois
Centre Hospitalier
☎ 54.55.66.33
Tours
Centre Hospitalier
2 boulevard Tonnellé
☎ 47.47.47.47

PRACTICAL INFORMATION   109

Tours
Centre anti-poison
☎ 47.66.85.11

Theft or loss
● Of car or personal belongings
Go to the nearest local or national police station, the *gendarmerie* or *Commissariat de Police*.
● Of passport or identity papers
Go to the nearest local or national police station, consulate or embassy, or administrative police headquarters, the *préfecture*.
● Of credit cards
Go to the nearest local or national police station or to the *Mairie* or town hall and immediately notify:
Diner's Club ☎ (1) 47.62.75.00
Carte Bleue (Barclaycard and Visa) ☎ (1) 42.77.11.90
American Express ☎ (1) 47.08.31.21
Eurocard (Mastercard and Access) ☎ (1) 43.23.46.46
After reporting the loss you will need a copy of the police's official report for a claim against your insurance on your return.

National Holidays
Administrative offices and most shops close on public holidays. If any national holiday falls on a Tuesday or a Friday, the day between it and the nearest Sunday is also a holiday.

Le jour de l'an New Year's Day, January 1
Lundi de Pâques Easter Monday, varies
Fête de travail Labour Day, May 1
Ascension Ascension Day, varies
Armistice '45 VE Day, May 8
Lundi de Pentecôte Whit Monday, varies
Fête nationale Bastille Day, July 14
Assomption Assumption Day, August 15
Toussaint All Saints' Day, November 1
Armistice '18 Remembrance Day, November 11
Noël Christmas Day, December 25

Shops
Food shops tend to open early, close at around midday for a lengthy lunch period, and then re-open in the afternoon for another four hours or so. Many will open on Sunday mornings, staying closed on Mondays instead. In France, lunchtime is very definitely the time for lunch and not shopping or anything else. The police stations close, so do the museums and major sites, the lorries leave the roads and the streets empty as the restaurants and cafés fill. This is, incidentally, the perfect time to make distance on the roads which become miraculously clear.

Market days
Amboise: Friday and Sunday morning
Azay-le-Rideau: Wednesday and Saturday morning
Blois: Zup Nord, Wednesday morning; Halle Louis XII, Saturday morning
Langeais: Wednesday morning
Tours: Sunday morning; boulevard Béranger, Wednesday and Saturday

Weather
Paris, Ile-de-France
☎ 46.65.00.00
Other *départements*
☎ 36.65.00 followed by the two numbers which represent the *département* (for example, Cher ☎ 36.65.00.18).
Average maximum temperatures (°C)

Apr	May	Jun	Jul	Aug	Sep	Oct
15	19	23	25	24	22	16

HIGH SPEED TRAIN (T.G.V.)

WHERE TO STAY

Out of season you can usually find accommodation en route and as the fancy takes you. The local Tourist Office, which is known either as an *Office de Tourisme* or a *Syndicat d'Initiative,* can provide on-the-spot advice and information on accommodation availability. However, if your visit coincides with the peak holiday period, you should always make advance reservations for accommodation.

The *Comité Régional du Tourisme* as well as the Tourist Board for each of the *départements* within the region (*Comité Départemental du Tourisme*) will supply, on request, specific brochures detailing camping, hotel and self-catering *gîte* accommodation in their areas, from which you can make your choice.

General information on the region can be obtained by telephoning or writing to:
Comité Régional du Tourisme Centre –
Val de Loire
9 rue St-Pierre Lentin, 45041 Orléans
☎ 38.54.95.42

Specific information on the individual *départements* can be obtained by telephoning or writing to:
Cher (18)
Comité Départemental du Tourisme
21 rue de la Chappe, 18000 Bourges
☎ 48.65.31.01
Eure-et-Loir (28)
Comité Départemental du Tourisme
place de la Cathédrale, 28000, Chartres
☎ 37.21.54.03
Indre (36)
Comité Départemental du Tourisme
Gare routière, rue Bourdillon,
36000 Châteauroux
☎ 54.22.91.20
Indre-et-Loire (37)
Comité Départemental du Tourisme
place Maréchal Leclerc, 37042 Tours
☎ 47.05.58.08
Loir-et-Cher (41)
Comité Départemental du Tourisme
Pavillon Anne de Bretagne,
3 avenue Jean Laigret, 41000 Blois
☎ 54.74.06.49
Loiret (45)
Comité Départemental du Tourisme
Carré Saint-Vincent,
boulevard Aristide Briant,
45000 Orléans
☎ 38.53.05.95

FRENCH CAMPING CARAVAN SITE

CAMPING

There are probably more camp sites in France than any other country in Europe, and they enjoy an excellent reputation. Living under canvas can be wonderful fun as many of the sites are more like holiday camps in their provision of on-site shopping facilities and entertainment, and with such activities as riding, tennis, canoeing, etc., all laid on. Amenities do vary though and camp sites are officially star-graded as follows:

*   basic but adequate amenities
**   good all-round standard of amenities
***   first class standard with emphasis on comfort and privacy
****   very comfortable, low-density and landscaped sites

All sites must display their grading and charges at the site entrance. For a family of four with tent, allow about 60FF for a * site and 150FF for a **** site per day. They must have roads connecting with the public highway, and be laid out so as to respect the environment, with at least 10 per cent of the ground devoted to trees or shrubs. They must also have adequate fire and security precautions, permanent and covered washing and sanitary facilities, linked to public drainage, and daily refuse collection. The maximum number of people per hectare, or about two and a half acres, is 300. However, at peak periods, when all sites are under considerable strain, there may be some relaxation in the regulations. Sites graded ** and above must have communal buildings lit (and roads lit for *** and ****), games areas (with equipment for *** and ****), a central meeting place, points for electric razors, surrounding fence with a day guard (night watchman for *** and **** sites). Sites graded *** and **** must also have washing facilities in cubicles, hot showers, safe deposits, telephones and good shops on or close to the site.

GITES

These are Government-sponsored, self-catering rural properties which can be anything from a small cottage or village house, to a flat or part of a farm. Reasonably priced, they are ideal for

WHERE TO STAY

GITE DE FRANCE

families travelling by car and offer an economical way to meet and mix with the locals. The owner will be on hand to greet you when you arrive.

A small membership fee entitles you to a fully illustrated official handbook and free reservation service from the official London booking office. Contact Gîtes de France, 178 Piccadilly, London W1V 9DB ☎ 071-493 3480.

More specific details for a particular location can be obtained by writing to the *Relais des Gîtes Ruraux de France et de Tourisme Vert* for each *département,* the addresses for which are listed below:

Gîtes de France du Cher
10 rue de la Chappe, 18000 Bourges
☎ 48.70.74.75 *(guide costs 25FF)*

Gîtes de France d'Eure-et-Loir
10 rue Dieudonnée-Costes,
28024 Chartres
☎ 37.24.45.45 *(guide costs 20FF)*

Gîtes de France de l'Indre
Gare routière, 36 rue Bourdillon,
36000 Châteauroux
☎ 54.27.58.61 *(guide costs 25FF)*

Gîtes de France d'Indre-et-Loir
Chambre d'Agriculture, BP 139,
38 rue Augustin-Fresnel,
37170 Chambray-lès-Tours
☎ 47.48.37.12 *(guide costs 35FF)*

Gîtes de France du Loir-et-Cher
11 place du Château, 41000 Blois
☎ 54.78.55.50 *(guide costs 28FF)*

Gîtes de France du Loiret
3 rue de la Bretonnerie, 45000 Orléans
☎ 38.54.83.83 *(guide costs 25FF)*

Chambres d'Hôte
Bed and breakfast accommodation in private homes, usually in rural locations. Local information on these available at the Tourist Offices.
Contact Gîtes de France Ltd, 178 Piccadilly, London W1V 9DB
☎ 071-408 1343 and 071-493 3480
In France contact the addresses above.

HOTELS

The French Government Tourist Office (FGTO), 178 Piccadilly, London W1V 0AL publishes a full list of hotel groups with details of booking offices in the UK as well as those French chains with whom you book direct. The official government star rating of hotels (Homologation Officielle du Ministère Chargé du Tourisme) is determined by the quality of accommodation, amenities and service. There are five grades, from * to **** Luxury and the prices quoted below are the minimum and maximum one might expect to pay per room.

- ****L   Luxury hotel (palace) 520FF upwards
- ****   Top class hotel 315–475FF
- ***   Very comfortable hotel 210–365FF
- **   Good average hotel 125–260FF
- *   Simple but fairly comfortable hotel 95–140FF

Prices are quoted per room, though a few may offer a reduction for single occupancy.
Just as at camp sites, hotel prices must be displayed outside and inside the establishment. Most hotels with their own restaurant expect you to take dinner when staying the night. Full board or *pension* terms, i.e. room and all meals, is offered

for a stay of three days or longer; half-board or *demi-pension* terms for room, breakfast and one meal are available outside the peak holiday period, and many hotels offer this in season too. Breakfast is not mandatory and you should not be billed for it if you haven't had it! Breakfast will be charged as a supplement varying between 15 and 77FF. When reserving accommodation, make sure the amount of *arrhes* or deposit is clearly stated, and ask for a receipt for any sum paid. When making telephone reservations, ensure that you state your arrival time, as hotels may re-allocate rooms after 7 p.m. If you find yourself delayed en route, make a courtesy phone call to the establishment, stating your revised arrival time.

A selection showing the variety of hotel accommodation on offer is listed below. Where possible, the British representative of a French hotel chain is given.

Café Couette
Guest rooms in approximately thirty private châteaux and distinctive homes in the region with optional evening meal.
Contact Café Couette Bed and Breakfast, 8-10 rue Isly, 75008 Paris
☎ (1)42.94.92.00

Campanile
Small, modern ** hotels. Guide provides good street location maps.
Contact Campanile, Unit 8, Red Lion Road, Hounslow TW3 1JF
☎ 081-569 5757
In France Campanile, 31 avenue Jean Moulin, Marne-la-Vallée, 77200 Torcy
☎ 66.62.46.46

Château-Accueil
Top-level accommodation as paying guests in private châteaux. See page 114.
Contact International Services Ltd, 7 Haymarket, London SW1Y 4BU
☎ 071-930 5551
In France Visafrance, 13 rue Saint-Louis, 78100 St-Germain-en-Laye
☎ (1)30.61.23.23

Châteaux, Hôtels Indépendents et Hostelleries d'Atmosphère
Stylish private establishments, such as châteaux, hotels and castles, offering hotel-type accommodation and services, but unaffiliated to any overseeing body. The illustrated guide book includes a section on restaurants.
Contact M. Farard, BP 12, 41700 Cour Cheverny (no telephone)

Climat de France
Chain of 140 ** hotels throughout France.
Contact Voyages Vacances Ltd, 197 Knightsbridge, London SW7 1RB
☎ 071-581 5111
In France Climat de France, BP 93, 91943 Les Ulis ☎ (1)64.46.01.23

France Accueil – Minotel Europe
Family-run ** and *** hotels, many with pools. Guide lists 160 across the country.
Contact France Accueil Hotels (UK) Ltd, 10 Salisbury Hollow, Edington, Westbury BA13 4PF ☎ 0380 830125
In France 85 rue de Dessous-des-Berges, 75013 Paris ☎ (1)45.83.04.22

Grandes Etapes Françaises
Four of them in the Loire offering top-class accommodation.
Contact 140 rue de Belleville, 75020 Paris
☎ (1)43.66.06.06

Hôtels-Séjours-Tradition
Unique to the Loire region, this group is an association of 28 **, *** and **** hotels whose facilities usually include a park or

GITE DE FRANCE

WHERE TO STAY

MOULIN D'ETAPE

large garden, tennis court and pool.
Contact Comité Régional du Tourisme et des Loisirs Centre – Val de Loire, 9 rue St-Pierre Lentin, 45041 Orléans
☎ 38.54.95.42

Ibis ★★
240 ★★ hotels throughout France, a dozen or so of which are in the Loire region.
Contact Resinter, c/o Novotel, Shortlands, Hammersmith, London W6 8DR
☎ 071-724 1000
In France Ibis ★★, 6-8 rue du Bois Briard, Courcouronnes, 91021 Evry
☎ (1)60.77.27.27

Logis de France
Small and medium-sized family-run hotels often with restaurant. Ideal for short breaks or motoring holidays, these hotels are mostly ★ and ★★ and are almost always rurally situated. They provide very good and reasonably priced accommodation.
Contact FGTO, enclosing 80p stamps.
In France Logis de France, 83 avenue de l'Italie, 75013 Paris ☎ (1)45.84.70.00

Mapotel Best Western
160 ★★★ and ★★★★ privately owned hotels throughout France, a handful of which are situated in the Loire.
Contact Best Western Hotels, Vine House, 143 London Road, Kingston-upon-Thames KT2 6NA
☎ 081-541 0033
In France 74 avenue du Dr Arnold-Netter, 75012 Paris ☎ (1)43.41.22.44

Moulin Etape
Though only a couple are located in the Loire, this is a chain of thirty-six ★ to ★★★★ hotels with a difference – they are all located within converted mills. Some have restaurants, most are on or near water, all are beautiful. Their brochure details the history of each, price guide, exact location and address and telephone number for direct bookings.
Contact FGTO, for guide.
In France Moulin Etape, Auberge de Moulin de Chaméron, 18210 Bannegon
☎ 48.61.83.80

Relais du Silence
This chain of 139 hotels specializes in offering locations of total peace and tranquillity for restful stays, and there are a dozen of them in the Loire to enjoy. A multi-lingual brochure is produced as the chain operates throughout Europe.
Contact Hôtels Relais du Silence, 2 passage du Guesclin, 75015 Paris
☎ (1)45.66.77.77

Relais et Châteaux
Luxury hotel accommodation and restaurant guide, with about 10 locations in the Loire featured.
Contact FGTO, enclosing 80p stamps.
In France Relais et Châteaux, 9 avenue Marceau, 75116 Paris ☎ (1)47.23.41.42

LOISIRS ACCUEIL

Many *départements* in France put together fully illustrated brochures under the title Loisirs Accueil in which are detailed hundreds of local *gîtes*. Having received the brochure, one phone call will ascertain the availability of the *gîte* of your choice and the organization provides a free direct booking service. In addition, their brochures offer unusual and interesting short break ideas with accommodation arranged in local *gîtes*, hotels and camp sites. Further details on page 27.

CHATEAU-ACCUEIL

ANOTHER WAY OF LIFE...

Formed by a group of private châteaux owners, the Château-Accueil association offers visitors the opportunity to experience, as their paying guests, a style of living quite unique to France. You will be able to enjoy the surroundings and character of these magnificent buildings, not as a tourist inspecting empty, cold rooms, but as part of a real family home, your hosts often being descendants of the original owners.

In addition, many also offer or can arrange sporting and leisure pursuits locally, and the owners will be delighted to advise on their region, its history and traditions. However long you choose to stay, you can be sure that your hosts will be welcoming and make every effort to make your stay with them as enjoyable as possible.

Guest rooms may be within the château itself, in a separate private house or flat and can be either on a bed-and-breakfast basis or include evening meals. Reservations can be made direct with the owners, or through International Services Ltd, 7 Haymarket, London SW1Y 4BU ☎ 071-925 2455 and in France Visafrance, 13 rue Saint-Louis, 78100 St-Germain-en-Laye ☎ 30.61.23.23

❶ Château de la Beauvrière
Vierzon 7 km
Contact Comte et Comtesse de Brach, 78100 St-Hilaire-de-Court ☎ 48.75.14.63
Open Mar-Jan, closed Sun nights, 15 rooms. Evening meals.
Originally dating from the 12th century and with Renaissance additions, this is an attractive manor house which is now also a ** hotel. In peaceful surroundings, fishing, walks and tennis are offered.

❷ Château de Cinq-Mars
Langeais 4 km
Contact Mme Untersteller, Cinq-Mars-la-Pile, 37130 Langeais ☎ 47.96.36.60
Open Mar-Nov, 3 rooms. No restaurant.

Classed as a Historic Monument, parts of the property dating from the 11th century, the château once belonging to Cinq-Mars, the conspirator and enemy of Cardinal Richelieu, beheaded in 1642. Grass tennis courts adjacent to the moat, and further sports facilities close by.

❸ Château de Colliers
Chambord 5 km
Contact M. and Mme de Gélis, 41500 Muides-sur-Loire ☎ 54.87.50.75
Open Mar-Dec, 5 rooms. Evening meals on request.
Right on the banks of the Loire, and very close to a cluster of the major Loire valley châteaux, this 17th-century residence

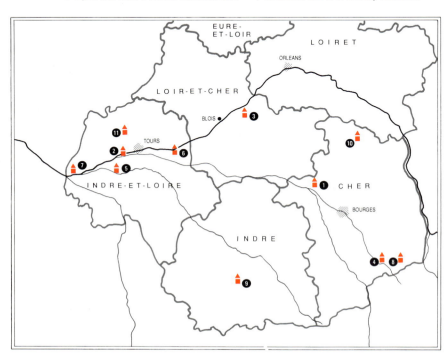

was constructed by the king's architect, Jacques Gabriel, and at one time was owned by the Governor of Louisiana. Hunting, golf and tennis locally.

❹ Château de la Commanderie
Bourges 36 km
Contact Comte and Comtesse B. de Jouffroy-Gonsans, Farges-Allichamps, 18200 St-Amand-Montrond
☎ 48.61.04.19
Open all year, 8 rooms. Evening meals on request.
Overlooking the Cher valley and close to the Forêt de Tronçais and George Sand country, this extensive building dates from two periods, the 11th and 19th centuries. Tennis, riding and golf are available nearby.

❺ Château du Gerfaut
Azay-le-Rideau 3 km
Contact Marquis and Marquise de Chénerilles, 37190 Azay-le-Rideau
☎ 47.45.40.16
Open Apr-Nov, 5 rooms. Evening meals on request. Elegant stone mansion set amidst woodland in the heart of châteaux country. Tennis on site and other activities available locally include ballooning, golf and riding.

VERRERIE CHATEAU

❻ Château de la Hubardière
Amboise 7 km
Contact Mme Sandrier, 37530 Nazelles
☎ 47.57.39.32
Open all year, 6 rooms. Evening meals on request.
Old hunting lodge overlooking large, stocked fishing pool. Furnished in period style, the building dates from the 18th century and is surrounded by woodland. Other local leisure activities include tennis, riding, golf and windsurfing.

❼ Château des Réaux
Tours 44 km
Contact M. and Mme de Bouillé, Le Port-Boulet, 37140 Bourgeuil ☎ 47.95.14.40
Open all year, 15 rooms. Evening meals on request.
One of the most attractive châteaux of Touraine's 'Vallée des Rois', this 15th-century building is of great architectural interest. Tennis, fishing, riding and golf.

❽ Château de Thaumiers
Bourges 36 km
Contact Vicomte and Vicomtesse de Bonneval, Thaumiers, 18210 Charenton-du-Cher ☎ 48.61.81.62
Open Mar-Nov, 11 rooms. No restaurant.
In vineyard and châteaux country, this is an elegant 18th-century manor house in the Berry countryside. Tennis and 4-hole golf course on the property with further sports facilities nearby. Helicopter landing pad.

❾ Château de la Tour
Châteauroux 30 km
Contact Duchesse de Clermont-Tonnerre, Rivarennes, 36800 Saint-Gaultier
☎ 54.47.06.12
Open all year, 10 rooms. Evening meals on request.
On the banks of the River Creuse, this building dates from the 14th century and enjoys the rural tranquillity of the area. The property hosts cultural events and can arrange for group courses in porcelain painting for eight to ten people.

❿ Château de la Verrerie
Aubigny-sur-Nère 10 km
Contact Comte and Comtesse de Vogüé, Oizon, 1870 Aubigny-sur-Nère
☎ 48.58.06.91
Open Mar-Nov, 11 rooms. Evening meals on request. Restaurant in the park.
A charming Renaissance château in a lakeside and parkland setting. On the 'Route Jacques Coeur', it was built at the end of the 15th century, the magnificent period furnishings adding to its appeal. The extensive grounds provide facilities for canoeing, tennis and riding.

⓫ Manoir du Grand Martigny
Tours 5 km
Contact M. and Mme Desmaris, Vallières, 37230 Fondettes ☎ 47.42.29.87
Open Mar-Nov, 5 rooms.
Lovely manor house in large parkland, close to the major châteaux and vineyards of the Touraine. Tennis, riding and golf available locally.

THE GRAND MARTIGNY

ATLAS

Easy to handle and full of useful information, you will find this 26-page atlas of IGN mapping an invaluable travel companion.
It begins with a double-page general map of the region (scale 1:1,200,000) enabling you to identify all the towns and major places of interest as well as estimate the distances between them. Page references to the more detailed maps of the area (scale 1:250,000) are shown on the grid of this general map.
The legend on page 119 lists all the symbols used on the maps, particularly those denoting places of interest to the tourist: churches and châteaux, historical buildings and curiosities, panoramic views and natural features. A colour code is used on the maps to differentiate between sights judged to be 'an absolute must', 'interesting' and 'worth seeing'.
Beside each town listed in the gazetteer you will find the corresponding map reference. The gazetteer section also includes street plans of the main towns.
Used in conjunction with the rest of the guidebook, this accurate, easy-to-read map section is your key to the region of France you are about to explore.

LEFT THE OLD CANAL AT BRIARE
ABOVE FLOCK OF GOATS, INDRE-ET-LOIRE

IGN MAPS

As the French saying goes: 'He who travels far cares for his horse...'. to which one could equally add '... and takes with him his IGN maps!' Essential to your travels in France, IGN maps, through their extensive and definitive range, meet every conceivable requirement.

FRANCE IN 16 MAPS
The Red Series
These maps are perfect for driving tours when getting to know a region. Scale 1:250,000 (1 cm = 2.5 km).

FRANCE IN 74 MAPS
The Green Series
Ideal for sporting use such as horse-riding, mountain-biking, canoeing, etc. Scale 1:100,000 (1 cm = 1 km).

FRANCE IN 2,000 MAPS
The Blue Series
These highly-detailed topographical maps are popular for walking, climbing and countryside exploration off the beaten track.

Scale 1:25,000 (1 cm = 250 m). From these have been developed a new practical series called the 'TOP 25': top for topographical and 25 short for the scale size 25,000. The particular qualities of these maps are their redesigned large format covering one specific tourist area (one 'Top 25' map replacing four or five conventional Blue Series maps). They carry a large amount of tourist and practical information enabling visitors to pinpoint with great accuracy the natural and other landmarks of the area. There are at present 90 titles with another 300 planned for the near future.

FRANCE FROM THE AIR
With their unique view of towns, holiday areas and sites of particular interest, the beautifully coloured IGN aero-posters and aerial photographs provide a detailed perspective of the French lanscape.

TOWN PLANS

	Motorway and express way	H	Town hall
	Motorway under tunnel	+	Hospital
	Main road with dual carriageway	▯ P	Police station
	Secondary road with dual carriageway	PF SP	Prefecture - Sub-prefecture
	Crossroads	✉ P	General Post Office - car park
	Main road	♥ ●	Theatre - Arts centre
	Secondary road	M i	Museum - Tourist office
		⚲ ⚲	Cathedral - Church
		⚴ ⚴	Abbey - Chapel
	Railway and siding	⚹ ☪	Temple - Synagogue - Mosque
	Narrow gauge track		
	River, canal	⚔ ⚔	Castle open to the public - Not open
	Ramparts, jetty	• ■ ⋰	Tower - Fort - Ruins
		∩	Cave Dwelling
		▨ 🚌	Passenger station - Coach station
	Perennial water	⚓ ⚑	Harbour station - Customs
	Non perennial water	≋ ⛳	Swimming pool - Golf
	Town centre	⛵ ★	Yachting harbour
	Urban area	⌣		Bridge, viaduc - Dam
	Wood, park	✈ ✈	Airport - Aerodrome

LEGEND

Motorway (1) - motorway standard (2)

Main road with separate roadways (1), Main roads (2) (3)

Secondary roads

Other roads : regularly maintained (1), not regularly maintained (2), Footpath (3)

Distances in kilometres (between ○ or two outlined cities)

Railways : double track (1), single track (2) - Station or stopping place (3), open to passenger traffic (4)

Boundary of region (1), of departement (2), of State (3)

Navigable canal (1), non navigable canal (2) - Salt pans (3) - Marsh or swamp (4)

Area exposed at low tide : Beach (1) - Rocks (2)

Wood

Airports : international (1), with hard runway (2), without hard runway (3).

TOURISM

Cathedral - Abbey - Church - Chapel

Castle - Castle open to public - Prominent building

View point - Curiosity

District of interest to tourists - Spa - Winter sports resort

Civil architecture (ancient house, bastide, covered market) - Rampart

Ancient remains - Interesting ruins - Memorial

Pilgrimage - Traditional festival - Museum

Military cemetery - Cave - Shelter - Lighthouse

Tourist railway - Rack railway - Aerial cableway, cable car or chair lift

Custom-houses : French, foreign

ITINERARIES

Drive

Walk

Cycling tour

Canal-river cruise

PLACES OF INTEREST

Not to be missed

Interesting

to see

Scale 1: 250 000

Kilomètres 5   3   1   0   5   10   15 Kilomètres

INSTITUT GÉOGRAPHIQUE NATIONAL

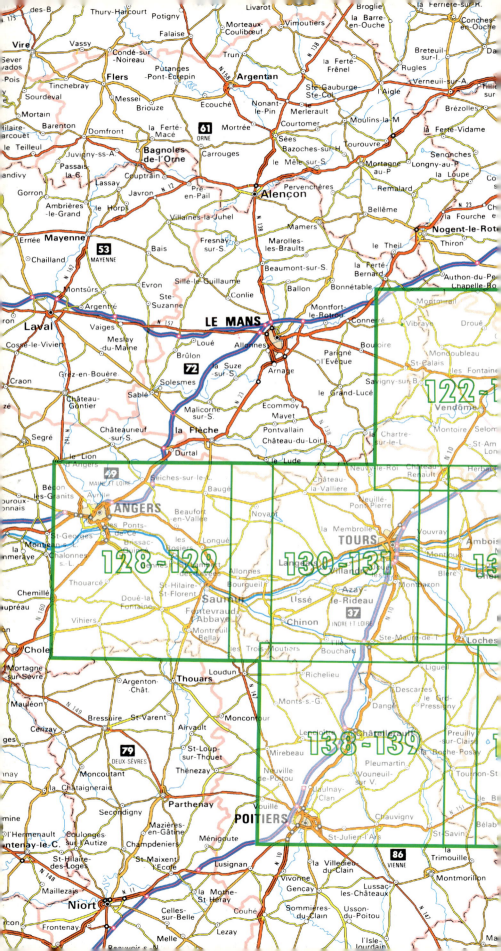

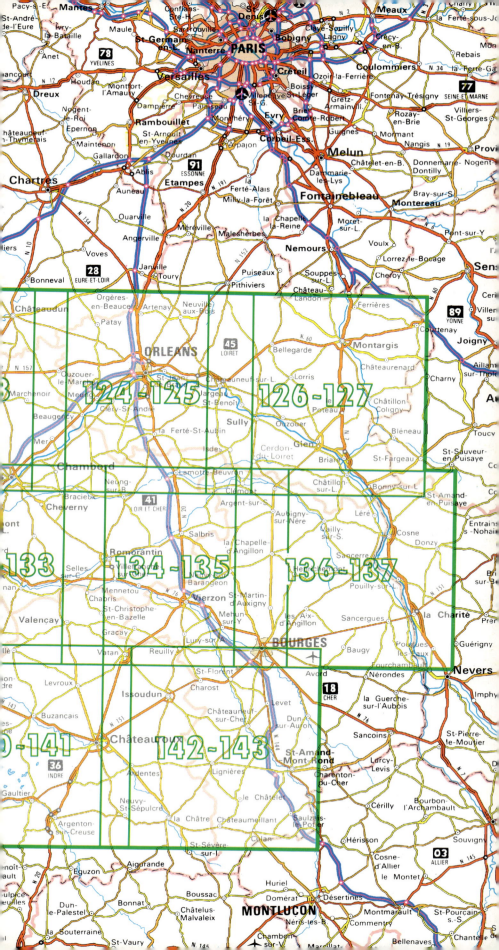

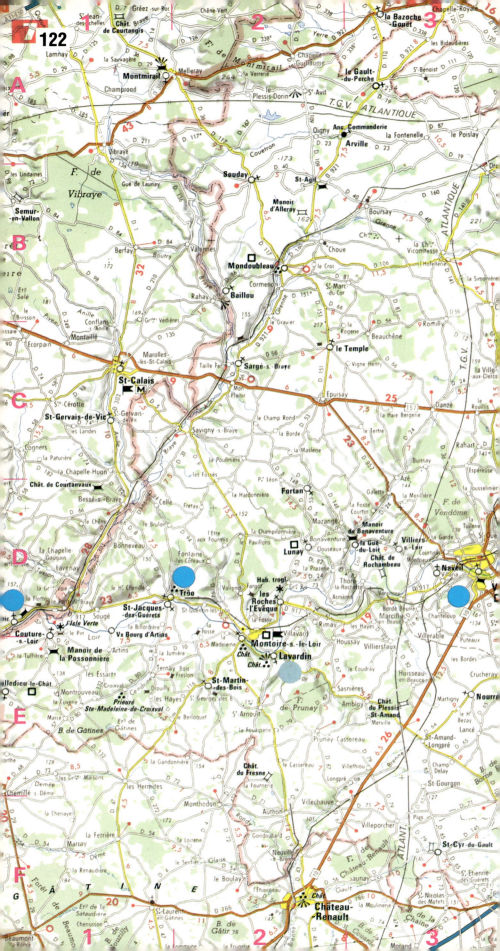

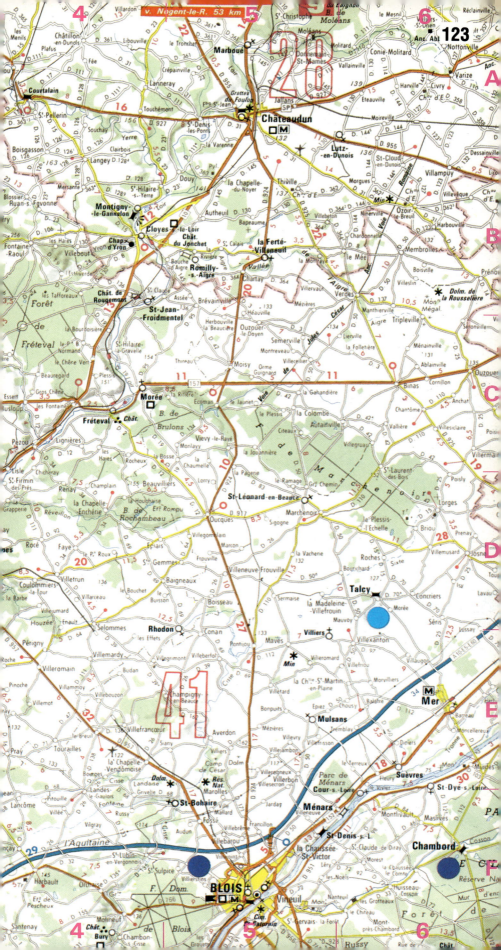

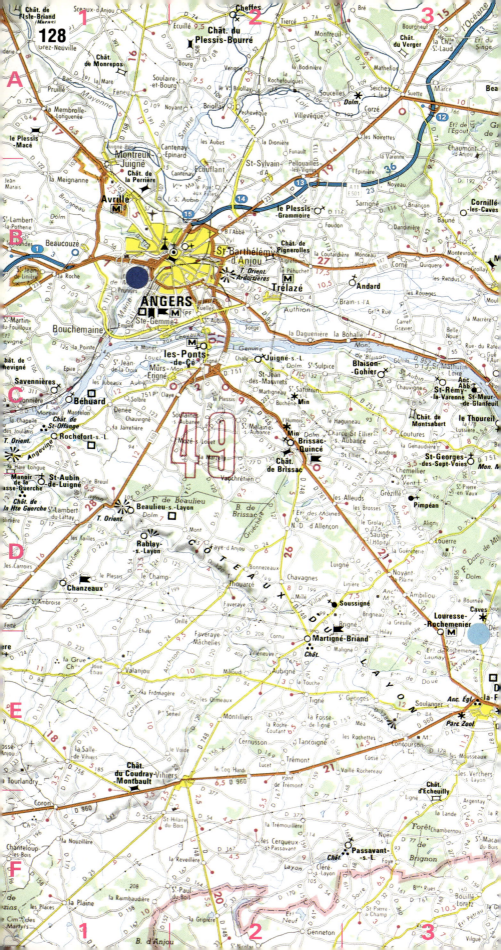

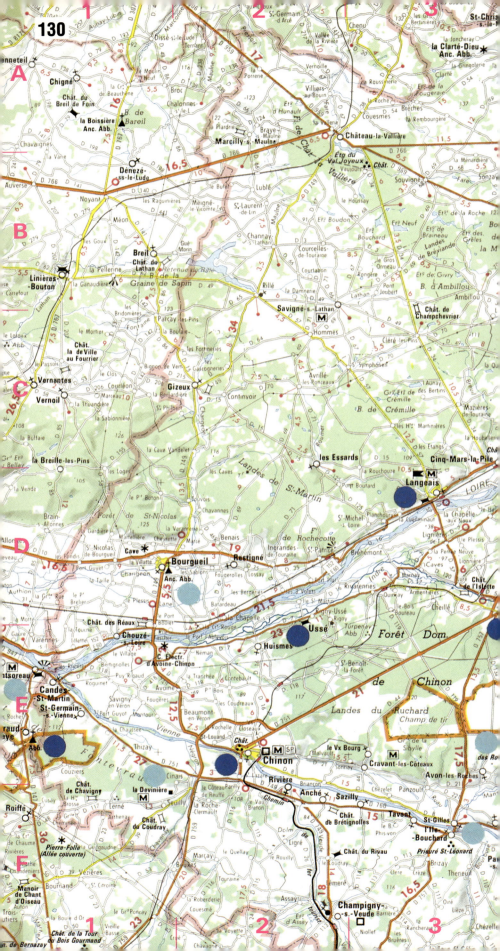

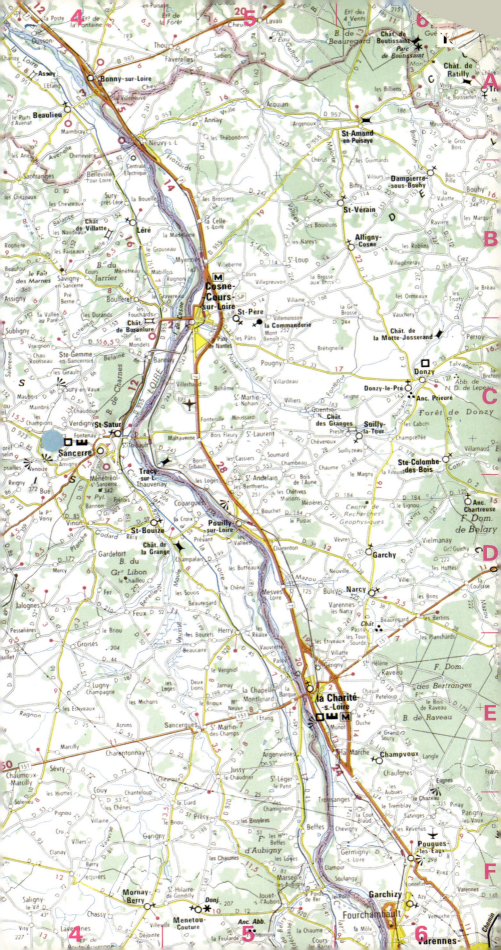

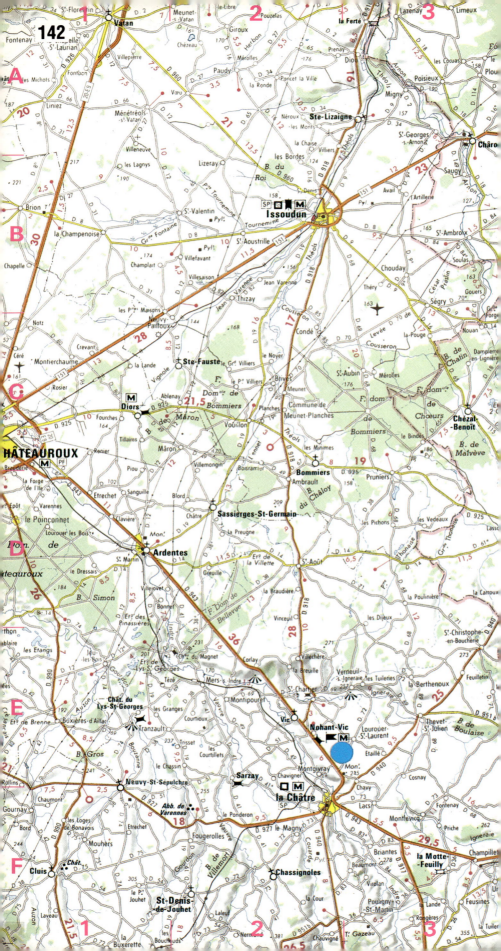

INDEX

Ainay-le-Vieil 53, 100
Amboise 14, 42, 66
Amigny 60
Angers 67
Angles-sur-l'Anglin 74
Artannes-sur-Indre 42
Argenton-sur-Creuse 68
Aubigny-sur-Nère 69
Azay-le-Ferron 7
Azay-le-Rideau 14, 40, 70
Azay-sur-Indre 42

Barres, Les 84
Beaugency 72
Beauregard 15
Beauval 48
Béhuard, L'île- 61
Blanc, Le 73
Bléré 42
Blois 15, 45, 74
Boischaut 7, 63, 100
Bouchard, L'île- 41
Bourges 51, 76
Bourgueil 40, 78
Bracieux 46
Brenne, La 74
Briare 50, 78
Bussière, La 50

Candé-sur-Beauvron 46
Chabris 47
Chambord 15, 45, 74
Chanteloup, Pagode de 8, 42
Chartres 80
Chartre-sur-le-Loir, La 44
Chaumont-sur-Loire 16, 46, 83
Châteaudun 81
Châteauneuf-sur-Cher 53

Châteauneuf-sur-Loire 51, 82
Châtre, La 63
Chaumont-sur-Loire 16, 46, 83
Chavignol 60
Chemery 48
Chenonceau 16, 42, 66
Cheverny 17, 46
Chinon 40, 83
Chouzé-sur-Loire 40
Clos-Lucé 66
Contres 46
Cormery 43
Courçay 43
Couture-sur-Loire 44, 92
Culan 100
Cunault 39

Devinière, La 13, 83
Doué-la-Fontaine 39
Dun-sur-Auron 100

Ferté-St-Aubin, La 17, 97
Fontevraud l'Abbaye 17, 39, 95
Fontgombault 74
Fougères-sur-Bièvre 46

Gennes-les-Rosiers 39
Germigny-des-Prés 51, 82
Gargilesse 69
Gien 18, 50, 84
Grand-Pressigny, Le 85
Gué-Péan 55, 94
Guerche, La 85

Issoudun 86

Langeais 18, 40, 88
Lavardin 44, 93

Ligny-le-Ribault 56
Loches 18, 42, 88
Lorris 90

Maintenon 90
Mehun-sur-Yèvre 90
Meillant 18, 53, 100
Ménars 19
Ménestreau-en-Villette 58
Mennetou-sur-Cher 91
Meung-sur-Loire 72
Montargis 92
Montbazon 42
Montgivray 63
Monthou-sur-Cher 55
Montlouis 43
Montoire-sur-le-Loir 44, 92
Montrésor 42, 93
Montreuil-Bellay 39, 94
Montrichard 42, 94
Montsoreau 38, 95

Nohant 13, 63
Noirlac, Abbaye de 53, 100

Olivet 50, 96
Onzain 46
Orléans 49, 97
Orléans, Forêt de 51
Orléans-la-Source 8, 50, 96

Pallauu-sur-Indre 54
Poncé-sur-le-Loir 19, 44
Possonnière, La 13, 44

Richelieu 98
Rochemenier 9
Roche-Posay, La 99

Roches-l'Evêque, Les 44, 93
Romorantin-Lanthenay 47, 100

St-Aignan 48
St-Amand-Montrond 53, 100
St-Benoît-sur-Laoire 50, 82
St-Cosme 13
St-Hilaire-St-Froment 39
St-Laurent-des-Eaux 72
St-Marcel 68
Saché 13, 42, 71
Sancerre 60, 101
Saumur 19, 38, 102
Savonnières 8, 40
Selles-sur-Cher 48
Sologne 47, 56, 69, 100
Sully-sur-Loire 20, 50, 103

Talcy 20
Thésée 56
Tours 40, 104
Tonçay, Forêt de 53
Trôo 44, 93

Ussé 20

Valençay 47, 93
Vendôme 44, 106
Verrerie, La 21, 69
Vesdun 101
Vierzon 107
Villandry 21, 105
Villaines-les-Rochers 42, 71
Vouvray 107